Speaking for Ourselves, Too

Speaking for Ourselves, Too

More Autobiographical Sketches by Notable
Authors of Books for Young Adults

Compiled and Edited by
Donald R. Gallo
Central Connecticut State University

National Council of Teachers of English
1111 W. Kenyon Road, Urbana, Illinois 61801-1096

NCTE Editorial Board: Keith Gilyard, Ronald Jobe, Joyce Kinkead, Louise Wetherbee Phelps, Gladys V. Veidemanis, Charles Suhor, Chair, *ex officio;* Michael Spooner, *ex officio*

Cover Design: Doug Burnett

Book Design: Doug Burnett

Manuscript Editor: Michael G. Ryan

NCTE Stock Number: 46236-3050

Library of Congress Cataloging-in-Publication Data
Speaking for ourselves, too : more autobiographical sketches by notable
   authors of books for young adults / compiled and edited by Donald R.
   Gallo.
     p.   cm.
    Continues: Speaking for ourselves. © 1990.
    Summary: Eighty-nine notable American and English authors of books
for young adults describe their life and work.
    ISBN 0-8141-4623-6 (paper) : $15.95 (est.)
    1. Authors, American—20th century—Biography—Dictionaries.
2. Authors, English—20th century—Biography—Dictionaries. 3. Young
adult literature, American—Bio-bibliography. 4. Young adult literature,
English—Bio-bibliography. 5. Young adult literature—Author-
ship. [1. Authors, American. 2. Authors, English. 3. Young adult literature.] I. Gallo, Donald R. II. Speaking for ourselves.
PS129.S644   1993
813'.54099283—dc20   92-44193
                                                        CIP

For Jane Christensen
in appreciation
of her dedicated contributions
to students, to educators, and to the Council,
especially at a time when its
publication program needed help the most.

Contents

Acknowledgments

My first round of thank-yous goes to the many teachers, librarians, and reviewers who responded so enthusiastically to *Speaking for Ourselves* when it first appeared. It was your appreciation of that collection that convinced me of the need for a second volume.

To Joan Atkinson, Patty Campbell, Betty Carter, Terry Gruener, Sandra Payne, Jill Smilow, and Diane Tucillo, whose judgments resulted in the final choice of which authors were to be included in this book, I will be forever grateful.

As with the first volume, I am thankful to the publicity directors and marketing people at many publishing houses—especially Tamu Aljuwani, Catherine Balkin, Laurel Barnard, Cynthia D'Altorio, Jazan Higgins, Nanette Knaster, John Mason, Anne Okie, Christopher Marsden, and Jennifer Roberts—for forwarding letters to authors, providing addresses, and sending me photographs when I needed them. Without your generous assistance this book would not exist.

Thanks also to Michael Spooner and the editorial staff at NCTE headquarters for your diligent, quality work in shaping the numerous pieces of this project into one attractive publication.

Above all, my thanks to the many authors who took the time to write about their lives and their craft for this volume. This is your book, in your words.

Introduction

Soon after the publication of *Speaking for Ourselves* in the spring of 1990, the sales, as well as the reviews and articles written about it, indicated that the book was filling a need for information about authors of young adult books. The value of the book was confirmed when the American Library Association placed *Speaking for Ourselves* on its list of Best Books for Young Adults in 1991.

In spite of the interest in that book—perhaps because of it—I kept thinking about all the highly respected and well-liked writers, such as Jeannette Eyerly, Cynthia Rylant, Elizabeth George Speare, and Alden Carter, whom we had not profiled in that collection, and about the newer writers, such as Annette Curtis Klause, Francesca Lia Block, and Gary Soto, who were suddenly making an impact in the field of books for young adults. The production of a second volume seemed inevitable; I just didn't expect it to be so soon. But then very early one winter morning I awoke with an overwhelming urge to start a second collection. I *knew* it had to be done. Right away.

As most writers can tell you, such an irresistible feeling—a compulsion (not to be confused with inspiration)—that you *must* do this book becomes a very strong motivator that can sustain a writer (or an editor) through the rough spots during the long and sometimes tedious process from conception to publication. And so it was with this book.

Selecting the Authors for This Volume

In determining the parameters for the earlier collection of autobiographies, we set an arbitrary goal of one hundred people, selected through a survey of past and current officers in ALAN, the Assembly on Literature for Adolescents of NCTE. The criterion for inclusion in the book was determined by the answer to this question: Who are the 100 most important novelists writing for young adults? From the hundred authors who were identified and then invited to participate in that first collection, eighty-seven sent in their profiles, along with bibliographies and photographs.

"I didn't realize there were so many people who write for teenagers," several readers of that book remarked. But those of us who devote a good portion of our professional lives to the field of young adult books know differently; there are dozens of other authors who were not included in that volume. But which authors should be included in the next group?

Desiring a slightly different perspective than the one provided by ALAN officers for the first volume, I sought responses this time from people whose connections were mainly with libraries instead of classrooms. Seven individuals served as valued informants in determining which authors would be invited to be part of *Speaking for Ourselves, Too:*

- Joan Atkinson from the School of Library and Informational Studies at the University of Alabama.
- Patty Campbell, former columnist ("The YA Perplex") for *Wilson Library Bulletin* and editor of the Twayne Young Adult Author series.
- Betty Carter from the School of Library and Informational Studies at Texas Woman's University and former chair of the American Library Association's Best Books for Young Adults committee.
- Terry P. Gruener from the Center for Educational Excellence at the University of Maine.
- Sandra Payne, supervising young adult librarian of the Staten Island Branch Libraries of the New York Public Library.
- Jill Smilow, sales and marketing manager at Candlewick Press and former Marketing and Advertising Manager of *The Horn Book.*
- Diane P. Tuccillo, young adult services librarian of the Mesa Public Library in Mesa, Arizona.

I mailed to each of those people a list of 153 names of authors whose young adult novels I was familiar with from my own reading or whose names had appeared with some regularity in journal reviews or in such publications as NCTE's *Books for You* or in textbooks such as Ken Donelson and Alleen Nilsen's *Literature for Today's Young Adults.* The seven respondents were asked to circle the names of those authors whom they believed were the most important ones on the list—those who should definitely be included in this second volume—and to underline additional names of authors who should be considered if there was room. (I was once again aiming for one hundred names.)

The names on this list, like those from the first volume, were limited to writers whose main output has been fiction. As a result, we omitted well-known authors of nonfiction (e.g., Daniel Cohen, Jean Fritz, and Milton Meltzer), those who do not write mainly for a young adult audience (e.g., Terry Brooks, Joanne Greenberg, or Stephen King), and poets (such as Paul Janeczko and Eve Merriam), even though teenagers constitute a good proportion of the audience for those authors' books. It was an arbitrary decision, but I hope a sensible one.

As occurred with my survey for the first volume, there were very few names circled by all respondents. In spite of the fact that every respondent was (and is) extremely well-informed, perceptions varied— sometimes severely—as to who is and who is not an important person in the field. Seen another way, we each are familiar with and admire authors who are completely unknown to others of us. This is especially true of some of the newer authors in the field. For example, two of the seven respondents identified Linda Crew as being one of the best in the bunch; two identified her as a possibility to include, two didn't note her at all, and one admitted to being totally unfamiliar with Crew's work.

I suppose that's to be expected, this group being, in a way, a reflection of the country as a whole. Some authors are known by a lot of people, some by a few, and some are almost completely unknown. (Last week while speaking to a group of about forty reading teachers and K–12 reading specialists about young adult books, I mentioned Gary Paulsen, one of the "hottest" authors in the field today, whose *Hatchet* was purported to have been the bestselling YA novel in 1989– 90. More than half of those educators had never heard of him!)

Only six times did all seven respondents circle the names of the same authors (out of the 153 names provided); two other authors' names were circled by six respondents and underlined by the seventh. Those eight authors, the most well-known and highly regarded of the lot, are (in alphabetical order): C.S. Adler, Lynne Reid Banks, Alden R. Carter, Brock Cole, Pam Conrad, Margaret Mahy, Elizabeth George Speare, and Robert Westall.

Further evidence of the inconsistency in respondents' familiarity with individual authors was provided by the fact that each of the respondents suggested additional names for my original list—adding a total of seventy-three more people! I formed those names into a second list and mailed that to all the respondents, asking them to follow the same directions (circling and underlining) as they had for the first list.

Using an evaluation system of two points for a circle and one point for an underline, I "scored" each name and then ranked them, as I had done for the first volume. I cut the list at ninety-six names, since there were sixteen names in the next ranking group.

I then sent a letter of invitation to each of those ninety-six authors, asking them to write a 500-word autobiography and to send me a list of their publications along with a photo, preferably a recent one (which was not an easy task for a few).

In addition, I once again sent an invitation to those dozen authors who had been invited to be a part of the first volume but who had either refused to participate or ignored my request a few years earlier. (In the intervening years, one of those authors—Frank Bonham— died.) Unfortunately, my renewed efforts resulted in the same responses from most of those authors—i.e., some ignored my letters once again, while others repeated that they did not do "this kind of thing." Two of those authors, however, said they were delighted to be included and subsequently sent me their profiles.

A few of the newly invited authors also chose not to participate in this book, either by ignoring repeated invitations or by flatly stating their intent to not send me their personal sketches. As a result, you will not find the autobiographies of several prominent writers in either this volume or its predecessor, among them Alice Bach, John Donovan, Deborah Hautzig, Janni Howker, R.R. Knudson, Julius Lester, Margaret Mahy, Patricia A. McKillip, John Neufeld, Meredith Ann Pierce, Christopher Pike, Daniel Pinkwater, Mildred D. Taylor, Rosemary Wells, Barbara Wersba, and Phyllis A. Whitney. Irene Hunt was too ill to respond.

In the end, I collected a total of eighty-nine profiles for this book.

Observations

An examination of the profiles in this volume reveals many of the same things observed in the first volume, as might be expected. Here again, most of the authors indicate their early and continuous love of reading; their valued skills of listening and observing; their often solitary, sometimes lonely, childhoods; and their early knowledge that they wanted to be writers when they grew up. Few writers give any credit to classroom teachers for either inspiring them or helping them develop their writing skills. There are exceptions, of course. (See the "Introduction" to the first volume for a more detailed discussion of these characteristics.)

As can be seen in the first volume, quite a few of these writers have been and still are classroom teachers, though many of them have worked at a variety of other jobs, the most extensive lists having been provided by Pamela Sargent and Theodore Taylor. Sargent says: "I've worked as a model, salesclerk, solderer on an assembly line, typist in a library, file clerk, receptionist, and taught philosophy classes at SUNY at Binghamton." Taylor says: "Variously, I've been a sports reporter, crime writer, merchant seaman, naval officer, prizefighter manager, movie press agent and production assistant, and, earlier, less exciting endeavors—delivery boy and chicken plucker."

The majority of these writers seem able to make a living from their writing and speaking engagements alone, though other evidence beyond this volume suggests that many of these much-admired writers do not sell enough books to support themselves solely on their writing. On the other hand, a few writers included here have become very well-off from the sales of literally millions of copies of their books, most notably R. L. Stine from his many thrillers, Ann M. Martin from her Baby-sitters Club, and Francine Pascal from her Sweet Valley High series, and their various spinoffs.

Although there are many similarities between these profiles and those in the first volume, there are also interesting differences between this collection and its predecessor. In this volume there seems to be a wider range of ages, with some authors—such as Francesca Lia Block— in their twenties, while others—such as Barbara Corcoran and Jeannette Eyerly—have been writing books for children and young adults for at least twenty years, longer than some of the younger writers have been alive. But their octogenarian perspectives on teenagers are surprisingly contemporary.

Another important difference is that the authors in this volume were born in a wider variety of locations. In the first volume, a disproportionately high number—nearly 30 percent—of the writers were born or raised in or close to New York City. Not so in this group. These writers are almost as likely to have been born in Oregon or Ohio or Missouri as in New York, coming from over half the states in the Union, including Hawaii. The largest percentage of American writers in this volume, though, were born in California—about fifteen percent of them. There is also a higher percentage of authors in this volume from the United Kingdom, with approximately eighteen percent of them having been born in England. That their books for teenagers are highly regarded in the United States is indicative of the interrelatedness of the British and American societies in the book world.

Another evident difference is the proportion of nonwhite authors here. In the first volume of *Speaking for Ourselves,* nine of the eighty-seven authors are African American or Hispanic or Asian. Only three authors in this volume are people of color. Rather than indicating any prejudicial attitudes on the part of the respondents, this result indicates the unfortunately small number of nonwhite authors who have been writing for young adults during the past twenty-five years. Most of the important nonwhite writers in this business were already included in the first volume. Readers should also be aware that two of the prominent authors invited to be a part of these two volumes but who chose not to participate are members of minority groups. If a third volume is ever produced, new writers of color—such as Rita Garcia-Williams—whose works are just now becoming known in the field will likely be candidates for inclusion, along with dozens of other authors who are currently not yet well-known. The low minority representation in the YA field continues to be a problem which needs to be addressed by educators, writers' groups, and publishing companies.

One of the clearest differences between this volume and its predecessor is something that is not evident in the pages of this book but which can be observed only in the original manuscripts that authors submitted: the use of word processors and printers. In the earlier volume, approximately thirty percent of the autobiographies appear to have been written by means of a computer. In this volume, more than three-fourths of the manuscripts appear to be computer-generated. What a difference three years make.

Lessons to Be Learned

In addition to the pleasure of reading about one's favorite authors or learning about the background of previously unfamiliar writers, readers of this volume and its predecessor have the opportunity to learn about the writing processes of these distinguished professionals. Teachers should find such information useful for reinforcing what they have been telling students about how to write or for restructuring their own lessons about writing. Student writers can utilize the authors' advice, some of which is spelled out directly, though some of it is only implied by their personal writing processes. Some of the wisdom gleaned from the autobiographies in this volume follows.

The Writing Processes of Authors

"Forget about inspiration," admonishes British writer Philip Pullman, author of *Ruby in the Smoke*. "Any fool can write when they're inspired."

He suggests that student writers remember the golfer "who found that the more he practised, the luckier he got; you'll find that the more regularly you work, the more readily inspiration comes."

Good writing is more likely to be the result of careful observation and extensive personal experiences, many writers assert. Theodore Taylor, author of *The Cay*, recommends "Watching, listening: hearing." Adrienne Jones advises: "Watch. Listen. Remember."

As for personal experiences, Willo Davis Roberts notes that she and her husband have "been in a rock slide in the mountains of California, were nearly washed over a cliff by a flash flood, and had a huge bear try to get into our trailer with us in Alaska," all exciting experiences which she has been able to work into her stories. And Robert Westall recalls his youthful years in England in his British fishing village of North Shields where he saw "Chinese laundrymen with real pigtails, lascar sailors jabbering in Punjabi, Sikh carpetsellers in green turbans, Norwegian fishermen drunk as lords, Maltese gangsters . . . [o]rgan grinders with real monkeys . . . murders . . . and bodies floating away down the river," scenes which he has "harvested" for his stories.

But young writers need not wait for such exciting events to occur in their own lives, as Cynthia Rylant's profile suggests. Her memories are filled with quiet days in "a forsaken but stunningly beautiful part of Appalachia." She focuses on the sounds and smells of those quiet days: "Birds and cowbells, the buzz of bumblebees, the baying of far-off dogs. Everything smelled good. Milk smelled good, and ripe tomatoes, bacon, and molasses. Rosebushes, honeysuckle, pine." "I soaked it all up," she says, "every last bit of it, everything I could take at so young an age, and when I grew up I began to ease these memories out, little by little, and I led them into books."

For most, observing isn't enough. Suzanne Newton says: "I love guessing *why* people do what they do. I love imitating voices, attitudes, personalities."

And if you feel that nothing exciting or interesting or special ever happens to you, there is always the game of "What if." Says Willo Davis Roberts: "Imagine what would happen to a person who saw a crime committed . . . or if your mother disappeared. . . . What would you do?"

Octogenarian Barbara Corcoran advises young writers to keep a journal in which personal experiences and thoughts can be recorded, though not very many of the authors in this volume mention keeping a journal themselves. Instead of a neatly-organized journal, Louise Moeri simply scribbles notes "on old grocery lists, used envelopes, and paper towels when that's all I can reach." "I'm a writer," she says, "who wakes up at 2:00 a.m. and scrawls a single word which, next morning grows into a scene, somewhat like those crystal gardens grow out of a dab of dead-looking crumbs in a bowl."

For others, the process of creating a book begins months, perhaps years, before the first chapter is begun. Humor writer P. J. Petersen, for example, says: "Before I write any words that will actually appear in the book, I generally fill a hundred pages or more with thoughts about the characters and the events. . . . When the characters and the action are clear enough in my mind, I sit down and write a first draft of the novel."

Most writers include a lot of themselves in their novels. "There are parts of myself in every book I write," notes Newbery Award-winning author Phyllis Reynolds Naylor. Marion Dane Bauer, a Newbery Honor Award winner, recommends that young writers "pay attention to the [stories] you're already telling yourself inside your own head." Francesca Lia Block, one of the newer writers in the young adult field, begins to develop her novels with an incident from her own life, she says, but then "I often look to a related myth or fairy tale for a more archetypal perspective. I add details from daily experiences that I have while writing, many mysteriously appropriate." She will "reach into myself to retrieve experiences and emotions I would often rather forget. But at the same time, writing has been a way to make sense of pain and confusion, a means of expressing joy, giving thanks, and connecting to others."

A few other authors use their writing to escape from the painful realities of their personal lives, as did the woman who chose the pen name of Louise Lawrence. "For days, weeks, months on end I could cease to be myself . . . let Louise Lawrence take over, travel time and the universe, create books from the visions that entered my head," she says. "I had to learn how not to exist so that the characters we wrote about could live instead of me."

Whether escaping from reality or simply thinking like a particular character would, it is essential for writers to get into the mind and feelings of their characters. Jeanne Betancourt says: "When I make up characters for my novels, I am inspired by my daughter, my former students, and the kids I meet when I visit schools. But when it comes down to writing the story and getting into the head and heart of . . . any of my characters—I have to become the character myself." Nancy Bond carries that a bit further when she says, "I become so involved in the lives of the characters I am creating that I can't let them go until I find out what happens to them."

Having a "love of great cats and a fascination with paleontology," fantasy writer Clare Bell chooses to write from the point of view of animals in her novels, like *Ratha's Creature*, set in prehistoric times. "Young readers can enjoy and learn from being inside a very different sort of 'skin,' " she says. This applies to young writers as well.

Speaking of a different sort of skin, Annette Curtis Klause, author of *The Silver Kiss*, admits that even though she works as a librarian during the day, when it comes time to write "every so often I turn into a werewolf."

Although much seems to come from within these writers, thorough outside research is essential to the success of most of their books. In fact, Newbery Award-winning author Elizabeth George Speare advises young writers to ignore the traditional advice of "writing about what one knows best." She recommends the use of the library to find out what you want to know through research, "a word that sounds forbidding to many people who have never discovered the fun and excitement of it."

For others, library research isn't sufficient. When Carolyn Meyer was writing *Killing the Kudu*, for example, she needed to understand the effects of a paralyzing spinal injury. Because her local library had almost nothing about it, she says, "I ended up working with the staff at a rehabilitation hospital, as well as talking with paraplegics." For another novel, she read books about the wilderness area where the story was set, went rock climbing, toured a music camp, visited a state penitentiary, and talked with an ex-convict familiar with prison life. To prepare for her "Hotline" series, Meyer took a month-long training course at a local mental health center, then worked a four-hour shift on the suicide prevention hotline once a week for a year.

But where do authors get their ideas in the first place? As noted earlier by Robert Westall and others, many of their ideas come from personal experiences and memories. Colby Rodowsky says her first book, *What About Me?*, was the result of her experiences teaching children in special education, and another book started after she had observed the interactions between a girl and her mother one day in a park. "Other people's lives have always fascinated me more than my own," says C. S. Adler, "so I still get most of the ideas for my stories from friends or acquaintances or items in the newspaper. . . . Of course, my characters' emotions have been mine at some time in my life. . . . I like fitting myself inside the skins of people very different from me and trying to see the world through their eyes."

Margaret I. Rostkowski, author of *After the Dancing Days*, says, "Family stories fuel my writing: by my great-uncles who were gassed and who caught measles in World War I, and by my grandfather who rode a motorcycle to teach school. I don't use the exact story but the feelings."

Writers who keep journals, as was noted earlier, can refer to them for ideas. Canadian science fiction writer Monica Hughes keeps an "ideas file" that she fills with "newspaper clippings of scientific facts and human interest stories." "Ideas are everywhere," she says, "and it is important to recognize them and to *write them down.*"

No authors in this volume suggest that budding writers should outline before they write, though a couple of authors, such as P. J. Petersen, imply that a kind of outline results from their initial writing of notes about characters and actions. Instead, many of these writers indicate that they start with a character (or characters) and a situation and just begin to write, watching what happens when the two interact. The most exciting thing about writing, says Ron Koertge, is "to see what characters will say and how they'll behave."

Just writing it down seems to be the preferred method. Sports novelist Thomas J. Dygard says: "I go as fast as I can from start to finish on the first draft." "Don't worry about writing the perfect sentence," says Jan Greenberg, "or you'll never get past the first line." Revision must then follow the creation of the first draft. Dygard says: "I rewrite, and rewrite, and rewrite."

Advice to Young Writers

First, who should be a writer? These authors do not debate whether writers are born or made, though many of them have noted that they remember having always wanted to be a writer. Surely, anyone can be taught to write more effectively. But individuals who become professional writers seem almost compelled to write. Suzanne Newton says: "I don't think you can keep a writer from being one. Lots of people have a talent for writing, but only a small group of these can't help themselves. They *have* to write." "Write about whatever burns in your mind," Adrienne Jones advises.

But whatever you write, several of these authors say, make sure you find enjoyment in doing it. "Write what makes you want to write more," advises Tamora Pierce; "write what's *fun.*" Gillian Cross says that you must entertain yourself, "Because if you don't, you're certainly never going to entertain anyone else."

Newbery Award-winning author E. L. Konigsburg offers three key lessons she has learned: "Write in a straightforward manner"; "Go from the specific to the general."; and "Ask big questions."

Although authors give a variety of advice to aspiring writers throughout this book, there is one point on which they all agree: to be a writer, one must first be a reader. Colby Rodowsky says, "Read, read, read. And read some more." Speaking specifically of writing science fiction—though it surely applies to writing any type of book, poem, or essay—author Douglas Hill says one must first be a reader of it. "Usually an addict. The reading, over the years, tunes and programmes the imagination."

Reinforcing what has been suggested throughout these autobiographical commentaries, Nancy Garden, author of *Annie on My Mind*, recommends a three-step process, what she calls "the three Rs of writing": "READ, WRITE, and REVISE." She also recommends writing something every day, "your diary, a letter, a book review." Ron Koertge says: "Write every day... and keep on writing." Alden R. Carter recommends writing on a regular schedule, "even if it's only twenty minutes a day—and rewrite, rewrite, rewrite." Similarly, Francine Pascal, creator of the enormously popular Sweet Valley High series, passes on the advice given to her by her mentor: " 'Keep going. Don't stop the flow. You can always come back on the rewrite.' "

One of the nice things about writing is that you don't need more than a pencil or a pen and a bit of paper to do it, and, Nancy Garden reminds us, it can be done just about anywhere.

From Carolyn Cooney, author of *The Face on the Milk Carton*, the advice is concise: "Write steadily, enjoy yourself, and never give up." Joyce Sweeney says: "Never be complacent with the quality of your writing and learn to ignore rejections." Sonia Levitin, similarly, provides three important qualities for a writer to have: "Perseverance, perseverance, perseverance."

Though sometimes it may be hard to do, the best advice to any writer seems to be, as Francine Pascal reminds us: "just keep writing."

Ways to Use This Collection

The most obvious use for these autobiographies, of course, is for the basic information each one provides about individual authors. Most readers begin by searching through the pages for their favorite authors to see what new things they can learn. But because these sketches are so brief and usually so interesting in themselves, many readers find them addictive. Like potato chips (but certainly more substantial), you can't stop after only one. So you read a few more for their entertainment value.

Beyond the simple pleasure these sketches provide, both teachers and students will find the bibliographies valuable. If you've read a title or two by one of the authors in this collection, the lists of their other publications provide the titles of other books to try next. Or if students have read a book that they are required to report on to the teacher or to the class, either written or oral, they can use *Speaking for Ourselves, Too* as a source of information about the author that they might be able to incorporate into their report.

For small-group or a whole-class activity with multiple copies of this book, students can be asked to read several profiles and look for patterns like those described earlier in this introduction—sources of ideas, writing processes, advice to young writers, etc. Evelyn Krieger, a reading specialist in Newton, Massachusetts, for example, has written about how she uses *Speaking for Ourselves* with junior high school students. She asks them to read a few profiles and look for characteristics that the writers have in common. She also encourages those students to "think about their own writing methods" in comparison with those of the authors they have read, asking questions such as "What's the hardest part about writing for you?" "What steps do you take when you write a story?" "What experiences in your life could you write about?" ("Using Author Awareness to Motivate Writers," *Reading Today* June/July 1991, p. 24).

More sophisticated students may want to look for similarities or differences between an author's style of writing in his or her autobiographical sketch and the style used in one of that author's novels or short stories.

However you choose to use this book, I hope you will find the varied voices of these distinguished authors engaging and insightful as they speak for themselves.

C. S. Adler

I suspect all writers of fiction do more living inside their own heads than in the world outside. As an only child growing up in the boroughs of New York City, real life seemed dull to me compared to the stories I was imagining.

It all started with reading. I submerged myself into the lives of the characters in the books I read, and I swam through the library shelves reading indiscriminately—as long as it was fiction. I read a book a day, and when my friends called me out in the streets to play potsy or war or stoop ball, I wouldn't go until I'd finished the last chapter of the book in hand.

Other people's lives have always fascinated me more than my own, so I still get most of the ideas for my stories from friends or acquaintances or items in the newspaper, rather than from my personal experiences. Of course, my characters' emotions have been mine at some time in my life. I don't think I could write about something I couldn't feel. But I like fitting myself inside the skins of people very different from me and trying to see the world through their eyes. That way I get to be funny and brave and wise—whatever I'd like to be and am not. To see the world from another's perspective makes writing fiction endlessly interesting for me.

I never thought of being anything but a writer. I was a too tall, too shy, too serious girl who listened a lot and didn't say much. The only talent I showed at all was for writing. I wrote for fun, made stories for myself from the age of seven on, and got my first rejection slips when I was in my teens. I kept writing novels and short stories while I went to Hunter High School and Hunter College in Manhattan, graduated, got married, worked in advertising, and stayed home to raise three children.

By the time I became a sixth- and eighth-grade English teacher in upstate New York, I was in my middle thirties and felt like a total failure as a writer. Sure, I had seventeen published teenage love stories to my credit, but no book of mine was on a library shelf. I was ready to give up the old dream and concentrate on being the best English teacher I could be. I even stopped writing, or thought I had. But somehow the habit of capturing life in words on paper wouldn't leave me, and I found myself writing bits of "poetry" and scenes that might be part of a book. I wrote while I was in bus stations or on vacations or waiting for my children to finish some lesson I'd chauffeured them to.

Finally, in my middle forties, I wrote a book about children called *Magic of the Glits*. I wrote it on a sand dune in Cape Cod while I was waiting for my husband to finish surfcasting. I wrote it for myself for fun, to pass the time, because writing was what I did. That book eventually—not easily—was published, and I quit teaching and became a full-time children's book author. I did it, and it only took me half a lifetime, but I still feel tremendously lucky to be earning a living doing what I love best to do, to have my books on library shelves, to get letters from kids who like what I write, to be the novelist I dreamed of becoming when I was a child.

Bibliography

Books for Young Adults

1981	*Down by the River*
1982	*The Evidence That Wasn't There*
1983	*The Shell Lady's Daughter*
1983	*Roadside Valentine*
1984	*Shadows on Little Reef Bay*
1984	*Fly Free*
1985	*Binding Ties*
1985	*With Westie and the Tin Man*
1986	*Kiss the Clown*
1988	*If You Need Me*
1991	*A Tribe for Lexi*
1992	*Tuna Fish Thanksgiving*

Books for Younger Readers

1979	*The Magic of the Glits*
1979	*The Silver Coach*

Vivien Alcock

I can't remember much about my early childhood. I have been told that a family friend dropped me into the sea when I was a baby. On purpose. He was testing his theory that this was the best way to teach children to swim—catch them early, toss them in, and away they'll go, like fish. He was wrong; I sank to the bottom like a stone.

This and other adventures happened to me before I had learned to talk. It must have been very frustrating. Perhaps this is why I have become a writer, so that I can tell my own stories instead of having to wait for other people to tell them for me.

I was the youngest of three sisters, born in a small seaside town in the south of England, some time ago, when the summers were always long and hot. The paint blistered on our front door. The pavements burned the soles of our feet. (We went without shoes from choice, not necessity. We were proud of our ability to walk barefoot over the sharp pebbles on the beach, and despised the day-trippers who had to wear shoes on their soft pink feet.)

Our mother was ill for as long as I can remember, in and out of the hospital all the time. When I was ten, she became terminally ill, and our father sent us to be looked after in Devizes, a market down in the country, miles away from the sea. We hated it there. We wanted to go home. But we had spent all our pocket money and could not afford to run away. Besides, where could we go? Our home was no longer there.

I often think of that time when I am writing. What surprises me is that my memories of it are by no means all miserable ones. Children are fortunately resilient. Even in bad times, they can find for themselves moments of happiness: a ginger and white cat purring on their bed, a pond full of tadpoles, a new friend.

When I left school, I studied at the Oxford School of Art for two years, but volunteered for the army before I had finished my course. It was at the time of the Second World War, and things were going badly for us. I have never regretted the impulse that took me into the recruiting centre. My joining the army might not have affected the course of the war, but it completely transformed my life. I became an ambulance driver, serving in France, Belgium, and Germany. My husband, Leon Garfield, was in the medical corps, and we met in a Toc H canteen in Belgium. Here, talking over our coffee, we discovered that we both wanted to be either an artist or a writer—or perhaps (in his case) a sailor, or (in my case) an actress. Anything seemed possible to us then. We were very young.

As it happened, we are now both writers and I wouldn't be surprised if our daughter Jane, now studying to be a teacher, didn't turn out to be a writer too, one day.

Bibliography

Books for Young Adults

1980   *The Haunting of Cassie Palmer*
1981   *The Stonewalkers*
1982   *The Sylvia Game*
1983   *Travelers by Night*
1984   *Ghostly Companions*
1985   *The Cuckoo Sister*
1987   *The Mysterious Mr. Ross*
1988   *The Monster Garden*
1989   *The Trial of Anna Cotman*
1991   *A Kind of Thief*
1992   *Singer to the Sea God*

Books for Younger Readers

1986   *Wait and See*
1989   *The Thing in the Woods*
1991   *The Dancing Bush*

Lynne Reid Banks

As the Library of Congress ungallantly announces to everyone at the beginning of all my books, I was born in 1929. That makes me well into my sixties at the time of writing this.

When I was a child, I used to think my mother, a beautiful actress whom I adored, would shrivel up and become old on the day of her fortieth birthday. Luckily she didn't; in fact, she lived to her eighties, and I plan to do the same, only I don't smoke sixty cigarettes a day as she did. I plan also to be a *healthy* old lady and go on writing and having fun and adventures until the day I drop dead. I hope this will occur in a classroom in some far-off place, preferably somewhere exotic like India, Africa, or China, when I'm in the middle of an English lesson. Think what a stir it would cause! I'm such an exhibitionist, I really don't fancy dying tamely in my bed.

I'm not a trained teacher. I actually never had a college education at all, partly due to World War II, and partly to my own stubborn insistence that all I wanted in life was to learn to be an actress. So when I got back from Canada (where I spent the war years as an evacuee) I went to drama school instead of continuing my studies. Just as well, perhaps; I wasn't very bright, and the acting training, which didn't do me a lot of good in my stage career, was the best basis I could have had for everything I've done since— teachers are only frustrated actors, after all! And I do lots of speaking. But the main thing is that writing fiction, whether it's books or plays or short stories, is very close to acting, in a way.

How? Well, it's this business of getting into different, made-up people's heads and imagining how they feel and what they'd do and say. Of course it's far harder than acting. With acting, someone else has written the words for you. The director gives you the moves. And above all, you only have to get into the head of one person at a time. When writing a book, not only are you inventing it all yourself, but you have to keep head-hopping: one minute you're in the head of a young woman quarrelling with her father, next you're him, reacting to what your daughter has just said, then you might be the mother chipping in, and at the same time you're you, the "omniscient author," watching it all going on and narrating the action from a god-like point of view.

I do like playing God, though it's very, very hard work and there's a lot of responsibility involved (personally I don't think the real God takes His responsibilities nearly as seriously as I take mine or the world wouldn't be in this ghastly mess). I love to travel and I love to come home to my family and to my beautiful cottage in southwest England. But I can never sit still for long. I need adventures to keep me going. And adventure means taking risks. Every book, like every journey, is an adventure: there's always danger in it, the danger of it going wrong, dying on you, or being heavily criticised. The pain and fear of all that never stops.

Writing is like traveling alone: there's no one to rely on, or blame, but yourself. It's the best way really, the way that stops you ever getting old. I hope.

Bibliography

Books for Young Adults

1973   *One More River* (rewritten and reissued 1992)
1975   *Sarah and After*
1977   *My Darling Villain*
1981   *The Writing on the Wall*
1990   *Melusine: A Mystery*

Books for Younger Readers

1977   *The Farthest-Away Mountain*
1978   *I, Houdini*
1980   *The Indian in the Cupboard*
1984   *Maura's Angel*
1985   *The Fairy Rebel*
1986   *Return of the Indian*
1989   *Secret of the Indian*
1992   *The Adventures of King Midas*

Books for Adults

1960   *The L-Shaped Room*
1962   *House of Hope* (in the U.K. as *An End to Running*)
1968   *Children at the Gate*
1970   *The Backward Shadow*
1974   *Two Is Lonely*
1976   *Dark Quartet*
1977   *Path to the Silent Country*
1979   *Letters to My Israeli Sons* (nonfiction)
1981   *Defy the Wilderness*
1982   *Torn Country* (nonfiction)
1984   *The Warning Bell*
1986   *Casualties*

Play for Children

1991   *The Travels of Yoshi and the Tea-Kettle*

Marion Dane Bauer

The problem with writers being asked to write about ourselves is that few of us live lives worth writing about. We tend to be observers, not actors. Now, ask me what I have learned from watching, and that's different territory entirely. But then, if you want to know that, you can read my stories.

I was born on November 20, 1938, in Oglesby, Illinois, a small town in the Illinois River valley. My parents, my older brother, and I lived in the cement mill housing on the edge of town. My childhood was mostly solitary, even lonely. I played with my cat, wandered in the woods, read, made up endless stories. Especially I made up stories.

I grew up to do the usual things I was expected to grow up to do. I went to college, married, taught for a few years, first college composition and then high school English, had a son and a daughter. I felt a deep responsibility to children, and I opened my home to foster children and exchange students and worked with youngsters in trouble with the law. But always, in some not-quite-hidden part of myself, I was busy making up stories.

I wrote, too—essays, poems, book reviews, letters, journals— but rarely stories. What, after all, could I write? I was living such an ordinary life.

Then one terrifying day, I sat down at my manual portable typewriter on its rickety table in a corner of the bedroom in front of the blankest sheet of paper I had ever seen. All those years, all those stories. There must be one I could write. The story of a lonely child, perhaps?

That was twenty years ago, and in those years I have written that story again and again. It's about a boy or a girl (or even a cat), isolated, alienated, who runs or is sent away from home, then chooses to return again. The final moment is always one of reconciliation between my young character and a parent or parent figure.

I work very hard to make each story different from all the ones before. I have lived in Oklahoma, Missouri, Minnesota, England, and searched out new stories in each place. To gather fresh material, I've gone whitewater rafting in Colorado and spent a week on a small island in the Minnesota boundary waters, and next I'm going to Alaska. But still, my story will come, in the end, to the same place. It's the one I've been telling myself all along.

It seems to be my own small gift to the world.

If you want to write stories, too, begin by paying attention to the ones you're already telling yourself inside your own head. If you pay close enough attention, you'll discover the one story all the others will grow from. It's a little like discovering the goose that lays the golden egg.

It's a little like discovering the entire world right in your own heart.

May all your stories be golden! May your heart be rich!

Bibliography

Books for Young Adults and Middle Graders

1976 *Shelter from the Wind*
1977 *Foster Child*
1980 *Tangled Butterfly*
1983 *Rain of Fire*
1985 *Like Mother, Like Daughter*
1986 *On My Honor*
1990 *A Dream of Queens and Castles*
1991 *Face to Face*
1992 *What's Your Story? A Young Person's Guide to Writing Fiction*
1993 *A Taste of Smoke*

Books for Younger Readers

1987 *Touch the Moon*
1992 *Ghost Eye*
1993 *Cat Summer*

Clare Bell

PHOTO: STUDIO ONE PHOTOGRAPHY

My people were coal miners, shipbuilders, and engineers: practical northern English working folk. Not a writer among the lot, at least that I can find. Perhaps it was the women who carried the talent. My mother and her sisters certainly had a gift for anecdote.

Though I spent only my first four years in England, immigrating to California in 1957, I gained a sense of my background through my mother. She introduced me to tinned kippers on toast and later told me stories of German bombs dropping on Newcastle during the Blitz.

From my mother, I got a love of reading, a gift for language, and a sense of outrage at the excesses of the Industrial Revolution. Its shadow also fell on my father. As a child, he watched his brother die of tuberculosis, an illness that killed many miners. He sought a technical scholarship to avoid the fate of being "sent down the mine." Long after he became a successful physicist, that fear still haunted him, turning him into a closed, driven workaholic.

After settling in the United States, my parents divorced and both remarried. My stepfather, Don Steward, is a software engineer who was a Mississippi Freedom Rider in the 1960s. He and I marched in the early moratoriums against the Vietnam War and he supported me when I later participated in nonviolent civil disobedience.

Having inherited my father's demons, and having watched my mother struggle as the first marriage came apart, I came to feel that a technical career was the only way a woman could gain independence and respect. By the time I reached college age, this path was opening. I took it, first becoming a chemist, then switching to electrical engineering after taking the National Science Foundation's

"Women in Engineering" one-year program. In 1978, I got an engineering job.

Even though I got along well with my co-workers, I often felt like some odd sort of animal as the only female professional in an all-male department. Perhaps one odd sort of animal called to another. My love of great cats and a fascination with paleontology created the prehistoric background and feline characters of *Ratha's Creature*. My work suggested the theme of how the introduction of technology (i.e., fire) can disrupt a society. But it was my own emotion that drove the center of the novel, the coming-of-age tale of a gifted young female and her rebellion against a male-dominated clan.

With encouragement from science fiction writer Andre Norton, plus wise editorial guidance from Margaret K. McElderry at Atheneum, *Ratha's Creature* was published in 1983. It shared the International Reading Association's Children's Choice Award and was chosen for a CBS Television "Storybreak" adaptation. Other books soon followed.

In 1988, when I reached a staff level engineering position, the job versus writing conflict sharpened. A year later, I left the company. It was a terrifying decision, given my family background. With some savings and a partnership with fellow writer M. Coleman Easton, I plunged in. To keep my hands busy, I converted a 1970 VW from gasoline to nonpolluting electric (and am now driving "Lightning Bug").

In my books, I like to take an animal's point of view. Young readers can enjoy and learn from being inside a very different sort of "skin." If someone can see through the eyes of a wild cat, they will not destroy the animal or allow others to.

Advice to future authors? Let me say something that applies mostly to young women. If you have the opportunity to do scientific or technical work, take it. Don't shy away. Difficult as it was, my engineering career gave me skills, resources, and insights that made me a more capable writer.

Bibliography

Books for Young Adults
1983   *Ratha's Creature*
1984   *Clan Ground*

| 1986 | *Tomorrow's Sphinx* |
| 1990 | *Ratha and Thistle-Chaser* |

Other Books

1989	*People of the Sky*
1992	*Daughter of the Reef* (with M. Coleman Easton)
1992	*The Jaguar's Kin*
1993	*Sister of the Shark* (with M. Coleman Easton)

Jeanne Betancourt

PHOTO: NANCY CRAMPTON

I grew up in rural Vermont. For many seasons of my childhood I lived across the road from a dairy farm. I spent hours upon hours playing in the fields, "helping" in the barns and hanging out in the big kitchen with our Swedish farmer/neighbors. Those years, I never thought of being a writer. But I wasn't planning on being a farmer either. I loved my tap dancing classes and wanted to be a Rockette at Radio City Music Hall.

Fast-forward through many years that include a move to New York City and seventeen years of teaching and you'll find me writing my first novel. It was thrilling to learn that I was a good storyteller—a spinner of tales—a writer of novels. And I've been doing it almost every day for the past twelve years. Besides novels for children and young adults, I tell stories through scripts for television and the movies.

One of the ways I get myself into a story is by reading and interviewing people on the subject I'm writing about. For example, to prepare to write *Kate's Turn*—the story of a girl from Oregon who comes to New York City to study ballet—I read autobiographies by ballerinas, interviewed young dancers, and watched them practice and perform. For my most recent novel, *My Name is ~~Brain~~ Brian*— about the class dummy who finds out that he's really smart—I spent many afternoons at a school for kids with dyslexia. And when I decided that Brian would learn everything he could about the Canada goose, I got to study them first.

When I make up the characters for my novels, I am inspired by my daughter, my former students, and the kids I meet when I visit schools. But when it comes down to writing the story and getting into the head and heart of Brian, Kate, Aviva, Elizabeth—or any of my other characters—I have to become the character myself.

14

Like Brian in *My Name is ~~Brain~~ Brian,* I have the learning disability dyslexia. But I don't think of it as a disability. I look at what my special abilities are—like having a sharply tuned attention to conversation (particularly the rhythms and emotional content of dialogue), strong visual memories, and the ability to imagine what it would be like to be in someone else's shoes (empathy). These are the abilities that I use in my storytelling. They're much more important for a storyteller than the abilities I don't have—being a good speller or a speedy reader.

Some people think that a writer's life is lonely. But when I'm writing a story I don't feel lonely because I am actively involved with lots of interesting people—the characters in my books. I love knowing that someday—in the private moment of reading—readers will get to know and care about these characters, too. If you are one of these readers, I hope you have as much enjoyment in reading my stories as I had in writing them.

Besides writing and reading, I spend my time gardening, drawing, and painting. My sporting life is pretty solitary. I've never been good in competitive sports, probably because I have terrible eye/hand coordination. So I swim, cross-country ski, do yoga, and ride my bike or motor scoot around the countryside.

A few years ago I moved into a house across the road from a farm, just like when I was a kid. And I still love to dance.

Bibliography

Books for Young Adults

1983	*Am I Normal?* (novelization)
1983	*Dear Diary* (novelization)
1985	*The Edge*
1986	*Between Us*
1986	*Sweet Sixteen and Never . . .*
1988	*Home Sweet Home*
1989	*Not Just Party Girls*
1990	*More Than Meets The Eye*

Books for Middle Graders

1983	*The Rainbow Kid*
1985	*Turtle Time*
1986	*Puppy Love*

1988   *Crazy Christmas*
1990   *Valentine Blues*
1992   *Kate's Turn*
1993   *My Name Is ~~Brain~~ Brian*

Nonfiction

1974   *Women In Focus*
1982   *Smile! How To Cope With Braces*

Francesca Lia Block

My parents always encouraged my interest in the arts and especially in writing. When I was still in the womb, they read poetry aloud to me and later told me Greek myths as bedtime stories. I began to write as a very young child. At University of California at Berkeley I studied English literature. My special interest was poetry, which I continue to look to for its rhythms, powerful concrete images, and succinct expression of emotion.

I wrote my first novel *Weetzie Bat* at Berkeley at a time when I was very anxious about my father's health and homesick for Los Angeles. After my father's death, I came back to L.A. and gave the manuscript to Kathryn Jacobi, an artist/illustrator who passed it on to Charlotte Zolotow at Harper. I have always treasured Charlotte Zolotow's work and *Mr. Rabbit and the Lovely Present* remains one of my favorite books of all time. Charlotte and Joanna Cotler completely understood Weetzie and encouraged me to write the sequels. Although Charlotte has subsequently retired, I am now working with Joanna on more books and feel incredibly fortunate to have such an open-minded, wise, enthusiastic editor who is also an amazing writer and artist (Joanna illustrated the covers of two of my books).

I tend to be obsessed with certain themes and images but rather than fighting this, I allow myself to explore them fully. I believe this is what can give writing a charge and intensity. One idea that continues to emerge in my books has to do with confronting darkness but believing in the enchantment of art and love. Out of this comes my style, which is a kind of magic realism.

I could compare my writing process to collage. I begin with an incident from my own life. Then I often look to a related myth or fairy tale for a more archetypal perspective. I add details from daily experiences that I have while writing, many mysteriously appropriate. After my first draft I usually better understand or even discover the underlying theme of the piece and rewrite accordingly.

As a writer I have experienced loneliness and isolation, and I have had to reach into myself to retrieve experiences and emotions I would often rather forget. But at the same time, writing has been a way to make sense of pain and confusion, a means of expressing joy, giving thanks, and connecting to others.

Although the writing process can be painful, it has taught me many life lessons. It is like dreaming—falling into a world of the most personal, resonant images and emotions that later can reveal things I might have been reluctant to face.

Bibliography

Books for Young Adults

1990   *Weetzie Bat*
1991   *Witch Baby*
1992   *Cherokee Bat and the Goat Guys*

Nancy Bond

There have always been books in my life. I grew up in a house full of them, and I live surrounded by them now. Some of the books are my own, but most are by other writers: people I consider acquaintances and friends because I know them through what they've written. I love stories. I love the feeling of connection they give me with worlds and people outside my immediate experience. My family makes fun of me because I hardly ever go anywhere without taking along a book, just in case. But, I say, you never know when a bus or a plane or a person will be late and you find you've got an unexpected half-hour—.

There isn't room to tell you much about myself (if you want to know more, you can read my books). I was born at the end of World War II, January 8, 1945. My father was in the navy, and my parents lived in Washington, D.C. As soon as he got out, they came north to Massachusetts, where he went to work for the Houghton Library at Harvard University. From the age of seven, with years out here and there, I've lived in Concord, Massachusetts, where I live now (and about which I've written two novels: *The Best of Enemies*, about Patriots' Day, our local April 19 holiday which celebrates the start of the Revolutionary War; and *A Place to Come Back To*).

I knew, when I graduated from Mount Holyoke College with a degree in English, that I wanted to work with books. Even though I'd always enjoyed writing, I didn't think then of becoming a writer. First I took a very secretarial job with a Boston publisher, and then another, slightly less secretarial job with a publisher in London. That was my first great independent adventure: working, and sharing a flat with a friend 3,000 miles from home. When I came back to Concord a year or so later and began looking for a job, a friend

19

invited me to work with her in the children's room of a small public library. I did and liked it, and a few years later, I went off to graduate school to learn more about being a librarian. The library school I chose was in Wales; I lived for a year in Aberystwyth, halfway up the Welsh coast.

I found, when I came home this time, that being a library director didn't suit me as well as I'd hoped. Instead, I began writing a book: *A String in the Harp*, my first novel, which was published in 1976. It's about an American family spending a year living on the coast of Wales. . . .

I've been writing ever since. It takes me well over a year to finish a book—often much longer. I find it hard work, and there are times when I'd rather be doing almost anything else, but I keep at it because, as I told you, I love stories and I become so involved in the lives of the characters I am creating that I can't let them go until I find out what happens to them.

When I'm not writing, I *still* like to read. (I don't see how you can be a writer if you don't love to read!) I work in a second-hand bookstore and I teach fiction writing at a Boston college. I like to travel—I get ideas for stories from places I've visited: England and Wales, Nova Scotia (*Another Shore* is set on Cape Breton Island), and the book I'm writing now takes place in Dunedin, New Zealand, where I've been twice. I like being out-of-doors and spend a lot of time walking with my large black dog Amos (there's a dog Amos in *A Place to Come Back To*—not quite the *same* dog). I enjoy spending time with friends, many of whom I've made through teaching, writing, and traveling. I haven't any children of my own, but in May 1990 my niece, Molly, was born, and ever since I've been happily collecting a library for her. I'm eager to share with her all the wonderful things there are to be found between the covers of books.

Bibliography

Books for Young Adults

1976   *A String in the Harp*
1978   *The Best of Enemies*
1980   *Country of Broken Stone*
1981   *The Voyage Begun*
1984   *A Place to Come Back To*
1988   *Another Shore*

Malcolm Bosse

PHOTO: LORI MACK

T hroughout my life I have maintained a romantic belief in the power of the imagination. Life traps many of us, but the imagination, as an instrument of change and escape, enables us to break out into the larger world of possibilities. I think this is especially true for the lonely and the disaffected who can find a way through art, literature, and music to make their lives defiantly better.

An only child, I grew up in Moline, Illinois, where I played football, ran track, and was lucky enough (as Richard Peck has claimed he was, too) to study Latin. Immediately after high school, I joined the Merchant Marine and commenced a routine of action that has taken me through years of military service, war, and worldwide travel, especially in Asia. My first novel was about the Vietnam War, based in part on my own experiences. Thereafter, I have alternated between writing books for adults and for young people. The subjects have ranged from China in the 1920s to prehistoric America, from fourteenth-century Europe to modern India.

Which is harder to write, a book for adults or young people? For me, the only difference is that the books for adults tend to be longer. The vocabulary I use is essentially the same for both, the plots are similarly intricate, the characters equally complicated. I don't believe in concessions to young readers in matters of style and difficulty of content. Some of the books I most fondly remember reading as a kid were beyond me in some ways, but the stretch it took to understand them contributed to their impact and lasting impression. But I do believe that narratives for either adults or young people must be vivid and hold the imagination or there's no sense in asking readers to go on with them.

Consequently, many of the settings for my books are exotic,

21

involve a lot of action, move rapidly, and say something important about the world as it was and as it is. The young adult book I am just finishing is about Borneo after World War I, and the next one will be set in fifteenth-century China. Yet I also believe that a writer can stay home, never travel, never have many experiences, and still create a rich world of fiction. Just look at Jane Austen. It all comes back to this concept of the imagination. If I have learned one thing during years of writing, it is that you must go beyond the facts into the heart of an experience and to do this you must go forward boldly, take chances, make mistakes, learn from them, and go forward again boldly, trusting your intuition. It is this sense of discovery through the imagination that keeps a writer writing.

Bibliography

Books for Young Adults
1979	*The 79 Squares*
1980	*Cave Beyond Time*
1981	*Ganesh*
1983	*The Barracuda Gang*
1987	*Captives of Time*

Books for Adults
1960	*The Journey of Tao Kim Nam*
1972	*The Incident at Naha*
1974	*The Man Who Loved Zoos*
1983	*The Warlord*
1985	*Fire in Heaven*
1989	*Stranger at the Gate*
1991	*Mister Touch*
1992	*The Vast Memory of Love*

Patricia Calvert

T he rugged hills that circled the home in Montana where I grew up were known by such sonorous names as Thunder Mountain, Monument Peak, and Old Baldy . . . the streams where I learned to fish were called Pilgrim Creek, Tenderfoot, and Big Timber . . . the gold and silver mines that dotted the mountainsides were labeled the Silver Bell, the Admiral Dewey, and the Goldbug. It was the place my teenaged father had moved his wife and two small children with the intent of "living off the land." It was a magical world in which to grow up, one in which lodgepole pines grew like arrows toward a sky that seemed always blue. . . .

But it was an isolated life, too, and two favorite pastimes that my brother John and I shared (he was my only playmate) were reading and storytelling. We were lucky to have had a mother who was a lively storyteller herself, and she never tired of entertaining us with sad and funny (sometimes outrageous!) tales about the Irish family of ten children in which she'd been raised.

She also read to us—a kerosene lamp provided our light—but we weren't treated to traditional children's classics. Instead, she read to us a crazy assortment of love stories, detective yarns, and adventure sagas from the popular magazines of the day, magazines that had been given to us by relatives who pitied our solitary way of life.

By the time I was ten years old, I knew that someday I'd like to be a writer myself, but years were to pass before I was able to write the kind of books I dreamed about writing. I grew up and left the mountains . . . went to college . . . married, then went to work . . . had two children of my own . . . even became a grandmother! Finally, my husband and I bought a small place in the country, and once again I found myself living off the land, somewhat as my parents had done so many years before.

A familiar and liberating "sense of place" came back to me, and in a fit of creative enthusiasm I converted an old chicken coop into a writing room and began to write. Half-forgotten stories my mother had told my brother and me came back to haunt me . . . I recalled stories from my own childhood and from my children's lives . . . and when my first book, *The Snowbird*, was published, I hoped that I would be able to communicate to my readers what, over time, had come to be my philosophy—that no matter how young or old one is, it is important to be able to say to oneself *I am accountable.*

It has been suggested to me that now that I've written several children's books, I might want to try "a real book"; that is, one for adults. Not likely! To write for and about children—and to write for and about the child in myself—is all I ever intend to do. No matter what color or gender or nationality we are, we are all emigrants from the same country: the land of childhood. I hope that I have been able to do justice in my fiction to the geography of that special place, which can be so beautiful or so bleak, and often both at the same time.

Bibliography

Books for Young Adults

1980	*The Snowbird*
1981	*The Money Creek Mare*
1982	*The Stone Pony*
1983	*The Hour of the Wolf*
1985	*Hadder MacColl*
1986	*Yesterday's Daughter*
1987	*Stranger, You and I*
1989	*When Morning Comes*
1992	*Another Good Summer*

Alden R. Carter

I wrote my first short story at the age of eight: Percy, a retired racehorse, pines to run a final steeplechase. His agreeable owners let him, but Percy—for all his will to win—cannot manage to clear the last fence and dies impaled on the sharp pickets. The end. "Beloved Old Percy" covered only three wide-line sheets and lacked a lot of details—e.g., riders for the horses. But, to my astonishment, it made my sister cry. At that moment, I knew I had to be a writer.

It took me a long time. Reading books and dreaming of becoming a writer always seemed more fun than actually trying to write. Books were prized in our home in Eau Claire, Wisconsin. Every evening, my father would put aside his serious book to read me a chapter of *Captain Blood, Showdown in Box Canyon,* or something similarly appealing to a child Visigoth. I'd go to bed writing tales of pirate raids and cowboy gunfights in my head. But little got on paper.

I was coeditor of my high school newspaper and one of two English majors in the navy ROTC unit at the University of Kansas. After five years as a naval officer, I left the service, intent on learning to write. Teaching seemed a job that would provide both a steady income and enough time off to learn the craft. Equipped with a teaching certificate from Montana State University and vast naïveté, I landed a job teaching high school English and journalism in Marshfield, Wisconsin. It didn't take me long to learn that teaching is an all-consuming profession. Much as I enjoyed my students and colleagues, I knew that I had to quit teaching or quit dreaming of becoming a professional writer. With my wife's encouragement, I left teaching after four years, once again intent on becoming a writer. Most of my family and friends thought I was crazy.

In my more lucid moments during the next two-and-a-half years, I could hardly blame them. My hours at the typewriter produced a fair amount of prose, but the mail brought only rejection slips. Finally, in the fall of 1982, I was offered a contract on my young adult novel *Growing Season*. Few moments in my life have been so grand.

My life has become very busy in the years since *Growing Season* made me a published writer. Between the novels, I write nonfiction for young adults on a wide variety of subjects. I also do a fair amount of speaking about my craft, particularly enjoying the time I spend with young people. For those who want to become professional writers, I always have the same advice: Write on a regular schedule—even if it's only twenty minutes a day—and rewrite, rewrite, rewrite.

I'm a happy man. My wife, son, and daughter share my love of books, travel, and the outdoors. I finally write rather than just dream about writing. I write for and about young adults because I like them; I find myself constantly impressed with their courage. Their stories are far more dramatic than the tales I once imagined about pirates, cowboys, and an ill-starred racehorse named Percy.

Bibliography

Novels for Young Adults

1984	*Growing Season*
1985	*Wart, Son of Toad*
1987	*Sheila's Dying*
1989	*Up Country*
1990	*RoboDad*

Nonfiction Books for Children and Young Adults

1985	*Supercomputers* (with Wayne LeBlanc)
1986	*Modern China*
1986	*Modern Electronics* (with Wayne LeBlanc)
1987	*Radio: From Marconi to the Space Age*
1987	*Illinois*
1988	*Colonies in Revolt*
1988	*Darkest Hours*
1988	*At the Forge of Liberty*
1988	*Birth of the Republic*

Aidan Chambers

I grew up on the outskirts of a coal mining town in the northeast of England. All the men in my family were craftsmen, mostly working in the mines. My father was a joiner (a finished-wood craftsman). The women were expected to stay at home and look after the men. I was an only child, and because there were few other children around me until I went to school, I was shy and a loner.

I was also a slow learner. Didn't learn to read properly till I was just nine, did badly with math, and wasn't much of a reader. Outside school, I loved the cinema (Laurel and Hardy were my heroes, and westerns among my favourite kind of films). The Second World War was being fought and this affected me deeply, of course.

When I was ten, we moved to another town, which I hated, but luckily I was sent late to the very good local academic high school where I was taken up by a teacher who turned me into a thoughtful and avid reader of literature. He it was who decided I should become a teacher of English, though secretly all I wanted to be was a writer. Since then, reading and writing literature have been my greatest passions.

This was the mid-1950s. Britain still conscripted its young men into the armed forces. I was consigned to the Royal Navy, where I spent a fairly miserable two years, before going to college in London, where I had a very happy time which ended with my becoming a teacher in a high school in a town on the North Sea coast, east of London. There I enjoyed myself even more.

I also became an Anglican (Episcopalian in United States terminology) and decided to see what it was like being a monk. So I joined a brand-new order that was dedicated to work with young people. For the next seven years, I was a monk and, at the same time, a teacher in a local high school in Stroud, a small town in the west of England. It was then that I finally started writing about the everyday lives of young adults (the ones in my classes).

These were the first books (plays and novels) of mine to be published. I've always preferred stories about contemporary life to any others, and I have never written any other kind except ghost stories, which I do for amusement. As much as the story itself, however, I'm interested in how the story is told—in the techniques of fiction.

Once started, I became so involved in writing that I couldn't go on being a monk as well. So I left the order and set up house nearby. I live in the same area still, a very beautiful part of England called the Cotswolds. Shakespeare's Stratford-on-Avon is on the northern edge.

After a while, I married an American who was working as a magazine editor in London. Together we set up a small publishing company, The Thimble Press, which produces *Signal,* a now-famous critical magazine about children's books, and other publications on that subject.

And so we have lived for the last twenty years: Me writing and editing novels and stories and plays, and Nancy editing our publications. It is the happiest life I can imagine and is exactly what I wished for when I was fifteen and first felt the urge to be a writer.

Bibliography

Books for Young Adults

1966	*Johnny Salter* (play)
1967	*Cycle Smash* (novelle)
1967	*The Car* (play)
1968	*Marle* (novelle)
1968	*The Chicken Run* (play)
1978	*Breaktime* a novel in the *Dance Sequence*
1981	*The Dream Cage* (play)
1983	*Dance on My Grave* a novel in the *Dance Sequence*
1987	*NIK: Now I Know* a novel in the *Dance Sequence* (in the U.K. as *Now I Know*)
1987	*A Haunt of Ghosts* (short stories)
1992	*The Toll Bridge* a novel in the *Dance Sequence*

Books for Middle Graders

1980   *Seal Secret*
1983   *The Present Takers*

Books for Adults

1969   *The Reluctant Reader*
1973   *Introducing Books to Children*
1985   *Booktalk* (essays)
1991   *The Reading Environment*
1992   *Tell Me: Children, Reading & Talk*

John Christopher

An only child of not very young parents (my mother was thirty-nine when I was born), I was transplanted in my eleventh year from rural Lancashire to Hampshire, a distance of some two hundred miles, into a totally different world. Customs, accents, props generally were new and bewildering: we traded up from kerosene to electric light. The move was caused by emotional shock within my small nuclear family, and the cultural shock was heavy, too. It was perhaps because of this that for several subsequent years I clung with a fanatical passion to the new-found magical universe of science fiction magazines from the United States.

Science fiction in those days depended heavily on science: it was a cardinal sin to flout scientific probability. It also depended on the prospect and promise of space travel. We expected and hoped for it within our lifetimes and viewed it as Columbus may have viewed crossing the Great Ocean. Scientific probability did not prohibit speculation concerning extraterrestrial life: our limited knowledge of the solar system, in fact, promoted it. We could happily daydream about a dying Mars, a young carboniferous Venus.

When I came to write science fiction myself, the conviction and the fascination were already waning. We knew more about the planets, too much for wonder. Scientific probability told us now that the vast spaces surrounding our teeming life-packed world carried only lifeless chunks of rock, and we knew the limitations imposed by Einsteinian theory effectively ruled out the exploration of other solar systems. (Writers came up with hyperdrives and tunneling through black holes: broomsticks would have done as well.)

By the time I was asked to try my hand at writing science fiction for young people, therefore, the future had lost its charm. I found the past more fascinating, and looked for a way to embroider that instead. So the Masters, stalking the earth in their ungainly Tripods, enhance their mind control of the conquered with a social sanction: they make people revert to the relatively easily controlled medieval system from the undisciplined chaos of capitalism. (I realized later they could have used Soviet communism instead, but fortunately didn't think of that at the time.)

This mix of past and future characterizes nearly all of my books for young people. The question of free will is also a continuing preoccupation, at its most extreme, perhaps, in *The Lotus Caves*. It's a kind of reversal of the Garden of Eden: the apple that tempts my characters grows on the Tree of Ignorance of Moral Responsibility.

I came to writing for children by accident, but stayed by choice. A distinguished English novelist, E. M. Forster, pronounced: "The novel tells a story. Oh dear, I suppose it does." The world was probably fragmenting anyway, but his comment didn't help. My own view is that if the novel doesn't tell a story, it's not worth writing; and young people, fortunately, still insist on being told them. This doesn't make the job easy, but it makes it a lot more satisfying.

Bibliography

The Tripods Trilogy

1967   *The White Mountains*
1967   *The City of Gold & Lead*
1968   *The Pool of Fire*

The Sword Trilogy

1970   *The Prince in Waiting*
1971   *Beyond the Burning Lands*
1972   *The Sword of the Spirits*

The Fireball Trilogy

1981   *Fireball*
1983   *New Found Land*
1986   *Dragon Dance*

Other Books

1969	*The Lotus Caves*
1970	*The Guardians*
1973	*Dom and Va*
1974	*Wild Jack*
1977	*Empty World*
1988	*When the Tripods Came*
1992	*A Dusk of Demons*

Patricia Clapp

My extremely happy life is divided into three areas: My large family, a thriving community theatre, and my writing. Putting words on paper is my favorite pastime. The theatre is my constant stimulant. My family is my greatest joy.

I was born in Boston, Massachusetts, in 1912. My father, Howard Clapp, died when I was nine months old. My mother remarried when I was four, and we moved to New Jersey, nearer to Manhattan where my stepfather worked. He was a wonderful father to me.

I was six when my stepbrother was born, and I was totally thrilled! He now lives in Canada, but we get together once or twice a year. We are close friends.

I went to a private school for girls, and was hopeless in every subject except English, French, Spanish, and horseback riding. Math was an utter mystery, but somehow I now manage my financial affairs very well. I never understood geography, though I have visited many foreign countries and enjoyed the travel. History was nothing but dates until I discovered, after I was grown, that history is simply the story of what people did. I can understand people!

After graduation, I took courses at the Columbia University School of Journalism. Under excellent professors I studied poetry writing, short story writing, novel writing—and more French and more Spanish. I enjoyed every minute of it and am not embarrassed to admit I have no degrees in anything.

At twenty, I married the brother of a schoolmate. He was eight years older than I, which never mattered. We had been married fifty-two years when he died.

From that intensely happy marriage came three children, ten grandchildren and (to date) eleven great-grandchildren, of whom my husband knew the first. A boy, named for him. He was delighted!

Over the years, from college on, I had some poetry and plays published. It was not until years later, when the grandchildren started arriving, that I wrote my first book, *Constance*. Constance Hopkins was an ancestor of my husband's. With that book, I discovered the wide world of historical fiction and, except for two books, *Jane-Emily* and *King of the Dollhouse*, I have stuck with it.

I lead a full, productive, and very happy life.

Bibliography

Books for Young Adults

1967	*Constance*
1968	*Jane-Emily*
1973	*King of the Dollhouse*
1974	*Dr. Elizabeth*
1977	*I'm Deborah Sampson*
1982	*Witch's Children*
1986	*The Tamarack Tree*

Bruce Clements

I write stories because I like trying to understand people and because it's a way of praising them. Of course, the people I'm writing about aren't actually alive and walking around in the world, but they seem very real to me while I'm getting their stories down. I spend two or three hours a day for about a year and a half keeping track of what they do and say and how they feel. In most cases I even get to like the terrible people in my stories. After all, they're human.

I think everybody has people in their heads about whom they could write stories if they wanted to. All you have to do is begin to ask questions. How old is Tom? What's Sharon's favorite piece of clothing? What three phone numbers does Carl know best, and when he dials them, who answers? Does Anna have a job? How important is money to her? How does she get along with her sister? And what does Max want more than anything else? That last question is very important. It's the engine of the story. If you know what your main character wants, and why he or she is going to have to struggle to get it, you're on your way.

In my last novel, Tom meets Anna and wants her to be his love forever. But there's another guy, an older guy, who wants her, too, and Tom has to move fast and be very smart because she's only going to be in town for two weeks. From the start, I knew what he wanted . . . Anna's love. I spent two years thinking and writing about him, and I never got tired of him or bothered by the amount of time I was having to spend with him to get his story right. (I spent a lot of time with Anna, too, of course; Tom wouldn't fall in love with just anybody.) More than anything else, writing means rewriting. You almost never get it right the first time. I want my readers to know exactly what Tom sees, and thinks, and feels, in a way that makes my readers forget about the words I write and get completely into the world in which Tom lives.

And now I've told you all I know.

Bibliography

Books for Young Adults

1967	*Two Against the Tide*
1969	*The Face of Abraham Candle*
1974	*I Tell a Lie Every So Often*
1977	*Prison Window, Jerusalem Blue*
1980	*Anywhere Else But Here*
1984	*Coming About*
1986	*The Treasure of Plunderell Manor*
1990	*Tom Loves Anna Loves Tom*

Books for Adults

| 1972 | *From Ice Set Free: The Story of Otto Kiep* |
| 1975 | *Coming Home from a Place You've Never Been Before* |

Brock Cole

PHOTO: TOBIAH COLE

I was born in a small town in Michigan and spent my first few years there. My grandfather was a dentist and a banker, who lost most of his money in the Great Depression. I remember him as old and frail, in a large house with two parlors and a crack in the dining room wall for which the railroad was held responsible. He would listen to "Mr. Keene, Tracer of Lost Persons," on a large radio which also gave us all the news about the war in Europe.

When I was young, children were generally swept out of the house in the morning and not expected to show up again before dark, except for meals. I don't think adults worried about us much. How wonderful that was! And, indeed, we seemed quite indestructible. I remember very clearly falling off a hay wagon once and having the heavy, steel-shod wheel bounce across my chest. I never told anyone. I wasn't hurt. I think miracles were more common then. I learned to swim in a dammed creek when I was four or five. There were no shallows. A person simply plunged in and dog paddled for dear life. We dug great entrenchments in the piles of earth at the County Barns, and in the summer sailed rowboats across a nearby lake, using sheets and bamboo poles for rigging. At one end of the lake was a swamp, and I sometimes saw there enormous gar fish and soft-shelled turtles sailing beneath the boat in the clear, amber water.

In the fall, just at dusk, there would sometimes arrive great flocks of migrating starlings, and they would roost in the tall elms and make such a noise as I've never heard since. Men would take their shotguns out into the streets and slaughter hundreds of the birds, that would then be swept into the gutters and cremated under great piles of burning leaves. My mother didn't approve of this, and would call for my brother and me to come in, but we resisted as long as we dared. I can still remember very clearly the fading light, the dark figures of the men in the middle of the road pointing their guns straight up, and the derisive chorus of thousands of invisible birds overhead. . . .

After the war, we moved from city to city, town to town. I went to six grade schools and three high schools, but didn't feel at all disadvantaged. Sometimes it was a relief to move. I was, off and on, a terrible student, particularly in those schools with any standards, and I enjoyed starting over in some new place. I'm very glad that I was born when I was, because I think I would be a very disappointing child today. I suppose I never really learned any discipline. Never really learned how to apply myself. I had a teacher who said I would never get ahead at this rate, and I suppose she was right. Here I am a writer and illustrator with no proper job experience at all.

Bibliography

Books for Young Adults

1987	*The Goats*
1989	*Celine*

Picture Books

1979	*The King at the Door*
1980	*No More Baths*
1981	*Nothing But a Pig*
1984	*The Winter Wren*
1986	*The Giant's Toe*
1991	*Alpha and the Dirty Baby*

Pam Conrad

PHOTO: SARAH CONRAD

My earliest memories are about books and words—little chairs and tables in the children's library room, my father standing in our basement apartment reciting the lines to "Frankie and Johnny" or "The Face on the Barroom Floor," and then late at night his voice reading *Moby Dick* to my mother, while I slept with Babar under my pillow and my own copy of *Winnie the Pooh*.

I began writing when I was seven and had chicken pox. My mother had given me some paper and colored pencils to draw with, but instead of drawing I began to write poetry that sounded a lot like A. A. Milne. From then on, whenever I had a fever, I would write poems. When I was twelve, my father published a private collection of them all, called *Tea by the Garden Wall*.

Through junior high and high school, I wrote mostly love poems and stories about girls who would perform acts of great sacrifice. After a year of college, I got married. During this time I wrote only in my journals or on stationery to send home news from Colorado and Texas where I lived with my husband. It wasn't until I was back in New York and my children were in school that I returned to college and thought of writing again.

I met Johanna Hurwitz at the Hofstra Writer's Conference in 1981 and decided to try my hand at children's books, as I was trying everything else from magazine articles to paperback romances. With Johanna's encouragement, I wrote a Beverly Cleary-type book called *I Don't Live Here!* and after twelve rejections I finally sold it to E. P. Dutton.

While I was mailing this book around, I began a new book. My earlier stay out West had introduced me to Nebraska, a place that both fascinated and terrified me. I had read Willa Cather, Mari

Sandoz, and, of course, the *Little House* books. I had a story to tell about a woman who moves from New York to the West—much like I had—and goes mad. But the story was too painful for me to write from her point of view. It wasn't till I found a child's voice to tell the story that it began to flow and *Prairie Songs* was written.

Since then, I have always written from my heart and not tried to imitate any other author. The picture books I write are very spontaneous and special, sort of midway between a poem and a hiccup. The original versions are usually written very quickly and then the thoughtful rewrites can take years.

Besides writing, I have discovered the joy of teaching writing. I believe that all we write comes *through* us, not from us, that we're channels of sorts for hundreds of stories that are floating around in the universe. And the greatest happiness for me is when, all of a sudden, little parts of my life begin to take on a strange, new significance.

I live in Rockville Centre with my teenage daughter, who, when she was little and I gave her paper to write poems, drew pictures. We intend to collaborate on a picture book one day, and we hope to become the "Judds" of children's literature.

Bibliography

Books for Young Adults

1986   *Holding Me Here*
1987   *What I Did for Roman*
1988   *Taking the Ferry Home*

Books for Middle Graders

1984   *I Don't Like It Here!*
1985   *Prairie Songs*
1989   *My Daniel*
1990   *Stonewords: A Ghost Story*
1991   *Prairie Visions* (nonfiction)
1991   *Pedro's Journal*

Books for Younger Readers

1987   *Seven Silly Circles*
1988   *Staying Nine*

Picture Books

1989   *The Tub People*, illus. by Richard Egielski

Caroline B. Cooney

I love books. I'm happy just looking at them, and I love buying, borrowing, and, of course, reading them. I also love writing them.

For me, writing is not hard. It is something I do every day for several hours and something about which I daydream for the rest of the day. My world is as populated by people I imagine as it is by people who exist.

When I was in elementary school, I was crazy about series books like *Nancy Drew* and *Judy Bolton*. I entered nursing school because of *Cherry Ames, Student Nurse,* and would certainly have become an airline stewardess like *Vicki Barr* had my bad eyesight not ruled that out. Later on, I fell in love with historical novels, and my own first four books were set in ancient Rome. Nobody published them. It's a good thing. They were awful!

It took me a long time to learn how to write well, and what I learned is that you must write steadily, enjoy yourself, and never give up.

My three children are my links to the world. At this writing, they are sixteen, twenty, and twenty-three. I volunteer in school and church music programs in order to be around teenagers more. I love the age group for which I write.

My daughters read constantly and read everything. My son finds reading a burden and for years dreaded any school assignment involving a book. It's given me a lot more sympathy and understanding for kids who don't want to read. Whenever I write I think about them—will a reluctant reader be glad he's chosen my book? Will he finish it? Will he write and tell me? Letters from my readers are the best part of any day.

I have sympathy, too, for kids who are not crazy about school.

I tried four colleges, disliked each, and never got anywhere near a college degree. But having read several million books (or so it seems: all of them are in my house—covering the walls, layered on the counters, lost under the couch, climbing the stairs), I am educated.

May you read with pleasure and may your thirst for knowledge never end.

Bibliography

Books for Young Adults

1981   *An April Love Story*
1982   *Nancy & Nick*
1982   *He Loves Me Not*
1982   *The Personal Touch*
1983   *Holly In Love*
1984   *I'm Not Your Other Half*
1986   *Don't Blame the Music*
1987   *The Rah Rah Girl*
1987   *Among Friends*
1988   *The Girl Who Invented Romance*
1988   *Camp Girl Meets Boy*
1988   *Camp Reunion*
1989   *Family Reunion*
1989   *The Fog*
1990   *The Snow*
1990   *The Fire*
1990   *The Face on the Milk Carton*
1991   *Twenty Pageants Later*
1991   *The Party's Over*
1991   *The Cheerleader*
1991   *Return of the Vampire*

Books for Younger Readers

1979   *Safe as the Grave*
1981   *Paper Caper*

Series

1985–86 Cheerleaders
         Trying Out
         Rumors

All the Way
Saying Yes

1986–88 Saturday Night
Saturday Night
Last Dance
New Year's Eve
Summer Night

Books for Adults

1980   *Rear View Mirror*
1983   *Sand Trap*

Barbara Corcoran

Compressing eighty-one years into five hundred words takes a bit of doing, but here goes: I was born in 1911 in South Hamilton, Massachusetts, a small town north of Boston and just a few miles from the sea. My mother, who had been a professional elocutionist before she was married, loved to read to me, and even before I could put words on paper myself, I began to make up stories. Being an only child, I invented a lot of my playmates. So, almost from birth, I knew I was going to be a writer, and no amount of practical advice, discouragement, and rejection slips ever stopped me.

I went to Wellesley College and graduated into the middle of the Depression, determined not to be either a school teacher or a secretary, the two professions most open to women at that time. Instead, I worked for the WPA Writers Project, and then in any theatre job I could find, because at that time I wanted to be a playwright.

World War II interrupted everything and gave me my first real job. When it was over, I headed for Hollywood, where most of my theatre friends had gone. I worked in a theatre there and then eight years for a branch office of Celebrity Service, which was fun and gave me some spare time to write. Later I worked at CBS Television.

All during this time I was selling small things—magazine pieces, short stories, some ghost-written movie documentaries, radio copy, whatever—but it never occurred to me to write for children until quite a few years later, when I had moved to Montana, received a master's degree at the university there, and had begun teaching college English in several different places—Kentucky, California, Colorado.

When I was offered tenure at a junior college in California, I

45

decided to turn it down and write full-time. My first book for children, *Sam,* had been published by Atheneum, and my editor Jean Karl had accepted a second book. Teaching and writing at the same time is hard to do, so I took the chance, moved back to my favorite state, Montana, and have lived here ever since, except for a year in Europe and England and a year in Hawaii. It hasn't always been easy, but I have always been glad I did it.

For quite a few years, I wrote four or five books a year, but now I am down to one or two. For almost all of my seventy-odd books I have had the same editor, and for years I have had the same agent, who have made life much easier and more fun for me.

I think anyone who wants to write needs first of all to read a great deal, all kinds of books in as many fields as possible. Keeping a journal is often helpful, if only because it gets one into the habit of writing a little every day. Learning to listen to other people helps a writer learn to write good dialogue and also often provides ideas for stories.

People always ask where my ideas come from—they ask every writer this question, I think—and it's a hard one to answer in a few words. Ideas for stories are everywhere; the trick is to look for them. Even someone you think is dull may have all kinds of things going on inside her that you don't see at a glance. Be curious, and that doesn't mean rude or intrusive, but noticing.

And above all, keep reading.

Selected Bibliography

Books for Young Adults

1968	*Sam*
1969	*Sasha My Friend*
1970	*The Long Journey*
1971	*This Is a Recording*
1972	*A Trick of Light*
1972	*Don't Slam the Door When You Go*
1973	*Silver Wolf* (as Paige Dixon)
1973	*The Winds of Time*
1974	*The Young Grizzly* (as Paige Dixon)
1974	*A Dance to Still Music*
1975	*The Clown*
1975	*May I Cross Your Golden River?* (as Paige Dixon)
1977	*The Faraway Island*

Linda Crew

S ince both my younger brother and I turned out to be writers, my mother enjoys reminding us of an article that once ran in the *Atlantic Monthly Magazine* wherein an East Coast author flatly stated that no writer could ever come from Corvallis, Oregon. He apparently felt the place was too pleasantly bucolic to stimulate creativity. What conflicts could a person possibly find to write about here?

He was probably just being cute, though. Anyone knows that if you've got people, you've got stories.

I'm not one to claim that from an early age I was determined to be a writer. During junior high in the early sixties, I wanted to be a folksinger. I thought the world centered around Greenwich Village in New York. But by high school, I had faced a hard fact of life—I couldn't sing. I decided to be an actress instead. I would go to Broadway! At the University of Oregon, however, my theatrical ambitions also evaporated. I didn't have a clue what to do instead. I asked my mother's advice.

"Well," she said, "how about journalism? You've always been a pretty good writer."

Life doesn't always work out so neatly, but in this case, I was lucky. I switched to journalism and loved it. We learned how to research, how to interview people, and how to sell what we wrote. We were encouraged to present the facts accurately and without fuss.

This was a good foundation, but looking back, my early inclination toward fiction is clear. In junior high and high school, many of my class assignments ended up in fictional form, and in college, even my news writing employed a suspicious amount of dialogue. I betrayed the fiction writer's weakness for always wanting to make the story just a little better than it really was. This is the approach I still take today—to have my work reflect real life and yet be shaped into the best story possible, for I feel that a powerful piece of fiction can often convey an emotional truth more compellingly than a strictly factual version.

After college I married Herb Crew, and we settled on the small farm where we still live with our three children.

In 1980, a family of Cambodian refugees came to pick cherry tomatoes and raspberries for us. As we became friends and I learned about their struggles to adjust to life in America, I began to feel that their stories needed to be shared with a wider audience. Eventually, after research and interviews with other Cambodians, all the stories formed the basis of my first book, *Children of the River.* It still amazes me how the idea for this novel was actually brought right to my door.

I never made it to New York as a folksinger or an actress, but now my work is being published there, and I'm happy with life here in my hometown. I feel confident that even here I'll find plenty of ideas for new books. Writers can come from anywhere!

Bibliography

Books for Young Adults
1989   *Children of the River*
1990   *Someday I'll Laugh About This*

Books for Middle Graders
1991   *Nekomah Creek*

Other Books
1993   *Ordinary Miracles*

Gillian Cross

PHOTO: LARK GILMER

All the time I was growing up, I thought I was preparing myself for a serious, intellectual career. I was born in England, near London, and I worked hard at being a model student and getting good grades on my exams. After school, I went to Oxford University, to study English, and then to the University of Sussex. I thought I was qualifying to be a university lecturer.

Luckily, lives don't go the way they're planned. There are always hiccups. In my case, the hiccups were my children (though I don't think they'd like to be described like that). We have four children, whose ages range from twenty-five to seven years old, and they all needed to be amused when they were small.

Different people have different ways of entertaining children. I make paper models and tell stories. The paper models are OK, but the stories work best, and I've always been a storyteller.

My first audience was made up of my younger brother and sister. Then I moved on to people outside the family. When I was thirteen or fourteen, I occupied the long train journeys to school every day by spinning a serial story for my friends—all about themselves and the people they had crushes on. And when I was a community service volunteer, waiting to go to university, I tamed a class of rowdy schoolkids with a ghost story.

So telling stories to my own children came naturally. But soon I found that I was enjoying that storytelling more than I enjoyed teaching people about what other people had said about the books I enjoyed. I was never cut out to be an English lecturer.

Instead, I did a variety of odd jobs. I worked for an Oxfordshire village baker who baked his own bread in a brick oven. I minded children for friends who were returning to work. I made appointments for people who wanted to see our local Member of Parliament—and I listened to their stories.

All the time, I was writing. It was five years before any of my books were published, but I don't remember worrying about that. Being published is exciting, but it's nothing to the excitement of when a story suddenly comes right and you can see how to make it mean more than just the words.

That's the test I'd set for anyone who wants to be a writer. *Do you enjoy doing it? Do you entertain yourself?* Because if you don't, you're certainly never going to entertain anyone else.

But if you do enjoy it—beware! If you let it get a grip on you, it might entice you away from the serious, intellectual things you intend to do. . . .

Bibliography

Books for Young Adults
1979   *The Iron Way*
1980   *Revolt at Ratcliffe's Rags* (in paperback as *Strike at Ratcliffe's Rags*)
1981   *A Whisper of Lace*
1982   *The Dark Behind the Curtain*
1983   *Born of the Sun*
1984   *On the Edge*
1986   *Chartbreak* (in the United States as *Chartbreaker*)
1987   *Roscoe's Leap*
1988   *A Map of Nowhere*
1990   *Wolf*
1992   *The Great Elephant Chase*

Books for Younger Readers
1979   *The Runaway*
1981   *Save Our School*
1982   *The Demon Headmaster*
1983   *The Mintyglo Kid*
1985   *The Prime Minister's Brain*
1986   *Swimathon*
1989   *Rescuing Gloria*
1990   *The Monster From Underground*

Jenny Davis

PHOTO: BILL RINGLE

My mother doesn't remember my birth and I don't, either. It was 1953, in Louisville, Kentucky. As a baby, I had bad health; my father says they thought I was dead three times because I quit breathing, but I survived.

My family was from the South but we lived in the North, in Pittsburgh, Pennsylvania. Perhaps because we were Southerners, we had a special obligation to the civil rights movement. I had seen "Colored Only" bathrooms and knew in my bones how wrong prejudice was. Some of my earliest memories are of marching, my whole family together, with thousands and even millions of other people, singing songs for equal rights.

Growing up in the now famous "sixties," I find I was very much a part of my times. I played with Hula Hoops and crouched in the proper position for air raid practice; I learned to twist with Chubby Checker, and watched Lassie, Ed Sullivan, and later the Smothers Brothers. We sang along with Pete Seeger and Joan Baez, then the Beatles and Bob Dylan. I was in fifth grade when JFK was shot. We watched the news with Walter Cronkite and read *Life* magazine. Soon, Vietnam began to filter into our lives. I remember the picture of the little girl running in terror down a path, burning alive from napalm. I still see her sometimes when I have bad dreams. I learned to use the copy machine at the Friends Meeting House and handed out leaflets against the war.

Like my character Livvie in the novel *Sex Education*, I, too, spent my fifteenth year in a university psychiatric hospital. The reasons she is there make up the story of that book; the reasons I was there, I'm still figuring out. In both cases it had to do with pain and caring.

53

I didn't go to much high school. Mostly I cut and went to the museum or the library or the park or practically anywhere but school. I hated it. Our school had gangs, race riots, and tight, vicious cliques. There were days when police patrolled with growling dogs. It was an overcrowded cage, and I escaped as often as I could.

The education I gave myself was haphazard and weak in many regards, but not worthless. Most importantly, I learned I could teach myself, and this has helped me all my life.

Eventually I went to a community college and found there all of the diversity of high school without the violence. I've come to believe that 99 percent of the quality of your education depends on your attitude.

Nowadays, I am a mother and a teacher and a writer. In my spare time I read books, write things like this, walk the dogs, dig in the garden, and visit with friends. I don't know how to sum up. This is a small piece of my life which for now, thank goodness, is still going on.

Peace.

Bibliography

Books for Young Adults

1987   *Goodbye and Keep Cold*
1988   *Sex Education*
1991   *Checking on the Moon*

Peter Dickinson

I was born in what is now Zambia, within earshot of the Victoria Falls, in 1927, the second of four boys. My father was a colonial civil servant, but died when I was seven, soon after we had returned to live in England. My mother (still alive) was the daughter of a South African farmer. In England I was raised on the fringes of the squirearchy (hence, maybe, the number of great country houses in my adult books, models of some place where I didn't quite belong). I won a scholarship to Eton, did military service just after World War II, spent three largely wasted years at Cambridge, and was offered (with a good deal of nepotism) a job on *Punch*, where I stayed for seventeen years, working as an editor but writing a lot of verse and some prose on the side.

In 1968, I published my first two books, an adult detective story and a children's science fiction adventure which I'd written to unblock the adult book when it got stuck. I left *Punch* that year, and since have been simply a writer. I have produced about forty books, some of which have been lucky enough to win prizes (and I mean lucky, for though few bad books win prizes, a lot of really good ones don't). I haven't much to say about my books. No doubt my life feeds into them at many points, but few are at all obviously autobiographical. I enjoy the work, except when it's going badly. Especially I enjoy the use of our language and the unleashed imagination, free to race around but trained to come to heel at a call. (Well, mostly.)

I married an admiral's daughter in 1952, and we had two daughters and two sons. She died in 1988, and in 1992 I married the American writer Robin McKinley. We live with three whippets in a large house in Hampshire.

Bibliography

Books for Young Adults

1970	*Emma Tupper's Diary*
1972	*The Dancing Bear*
1973	*The Gift*
1973	*The Iron Lion*
1975	*Chance, Luck and Destiny*
1976	*The Blue Hawk*
1977	*Annerton Pit*
1978	*Hepzibah*
1979	*Tulka*
1979	*The Flight of Dragons*
1980	*City of Gold and Other Stories from the Old Testament*
1981	*The Seventh Raven*
1983	*Healer*
1984	*Giant Cold*
1985	*A Box of Nothing*
1988	*Eva*
1988	*Merlin Dreams*
1990	*AK*
1992	*A Bone from a Dry Sea*

The Changes Trilogy

1968	*The Weathermonger*
1969	*Heartease*
1970	*The Devil's Children*

Books for Adults

1968	*Skin Deep*
1969	*A Pride of Heroes*
1970	*The Seals*
1971	*Sleep and His Brother*
1972	*The Lizard in the Cup*
1973	*The Green Gene*
1974	*The Poison Oracle*
1975	*The Lively Dead*
1976	*King and Joker*
1977	*Walking Dead*
1979	*One Foot in the Grave*
1981	*A Summer in the Twenties*

Berlie Doherty

I grew up by the sea, in Hoylake, and have always loved it. Now I live in Sheffield, a major city, and the beauty of it is that outside its bustle, there is wonderful calm, as it is surrounded by the most spectacular countryside. My first two children's books were set in Hoylake, the seaside town, and all my books since then (except *Snowy*) have been set in and around Sheffield, with the hills of Derbyshire in the background. *Granny Was a Buffer Girl* is very much about a Sheffield family and is set in the very house and street that my former husband grew up in. I know the Derbyshire farm where *White Peak Farm* is set, and *Dear Nobody* is in my part of Sheffield. Place is very important to me—I like to feel I know the landscape that my characters are walking in. But even more important than place is character. Storywriting for me is essentially about exploring an emotional landscape.

I knew I wanted to write when I was a little girl. My father used to tell me a bedtime story every night, and I remember thinking at the age of five that what I would most like to do would be to write bedtime stories for other people. My first poems and stories were published in a local paper, and I became a regular contributor until the dreadful day on my fourteenth birthday when I was told that I was too old to write for the children's page. I retired from writing then, and didn't write again for over twenty years.

What on earth did I do in that time? When I left school, I earned a degree in English literature at Durham University, and a post-graduate certificate in social science at Liverpool University. I became a social worker specialising in child and family casework, but left within a year to start my own family. When my children (Janna, Tim, and Sally) were small, my husband and I performed regularly in clubs as a folk duo, and when my youngest daughter started school, I went to Sheffield University to train as a teacher. It was in my first year of teaching that I started to write, often for the children in my class, and after two more years of teaching and two years of broadcasting I became a full-time writer. So I was gaining the most valuable experience during those "thinking years."

I like to call the process of writing "I remember and let's pretend." People always ask where the ideas come from. I feel they come from every minute of the day, from my active life as well as from my daydreaming inner life, and are just waiting to be explored.

Bibliography

Books for Young Adults

1988   *Granny Was a Buffer Girl*
1990   *White Peak Farm*
1992   *Dear Nobody*

Books for Younger Readers

1982   *How Green You Are!*
1983   *The Making of Fingers Finnigan*
1984   *Tilly Mint Tales*
1985   *Children of Winter*
1987   *Tilly Mint and the Dodo*
1987   *Tough Luck*
1989   *Spellhorn*
1993   *Ghost in the Garden* (poetry)
1993   *Big Bulgy Fat Black Slugs* (poetry)

Picture Books

1989   *Paddiwak and Cozy*
1992   *Snowy*

Books for Adults

1991   *Requiem*

Thomas J. Dygard

I've wanted to write ever since I learned to read. To me, reading has always been a great pleasure. It provided me trips to strange and fascinating places without leaving my chair, took me back in time and forward to the future, led me through exciting adventures, and introduced me to the great people of today and yesterday, some real and some fictional. To write, perhaps as well as some of those writers who thrilled me, was a dream almost as old as my life.

Wanting to write led me into journalism at an early age. While a senior in high school, I joined the sports staff of the *Arkansas Gazette*, then the morning newspaper in my hometown of Little Rock. I worked at the *Gazette* as a sports writer, city desk reporter, and correspondent through graduation from the University of Arkansas with a degree in history.

Shortly after graduation, I quit the *Gazette* to take a job as editor at the Institute of Science and Technology at the University of Arkansas, with the idea of working on an advanced degree.

But after six months, I knew something was missing, and when the Associated Press offered me a news job in the Little Rock bureau, I snapped it up. It was a career move that stuck. After two years in Little Rock, I worked in bureaus in Detroit, Birmingham, and New Orleans, and was chief of bureau in Little Rock, Indianapolis, and Chicago. At this writing, I am the chief of bureau in Tokyo, a post I've held for seven years.

All along, I tried my hand at fiction, off and on. I loved reading fiction, and I wanted to write it. I sold one short story—the first one I ever wrote—but then went years at a stretch without completing anything, much less selling anything.

Then one evening, left to my own devices alone in a motel in Champaign, Illinois, I decided to begin a novel, and I resolved to go all the way to the finish. I wrote the first chapter that night.

Needless to say, I did eventually finish the novel, *Running Scared*, the story of a college football quarterback with a terrible fear of injury. I had thought I was writing an adult novel. But when I reread what I had done, I concluded that I had a young adult novel, the sort that I'd read as a teenager.

After Morrow Junior Books accepted the manuscript for publication, the editor-in-chief, Connie Epstein, asked: "Can you do it again?"

I've been "doing it again" ever since, about once a year, with my thirteenth young adult novel, *Backfield Package*, just completed.

Virtually all of my fiction writing is done on the weekends, usually in the mornings. My method is simple. I go as fast as I can from start to finish on the first draft. Then I rewrite, and rewrite, and rewrite. I'm lucky that I enjoy every bit of the process. Writing for me is not torture. To the contrary, I approach fiction writing the way some might approach a round of golf—fun.

All of my novels have been sports stories of one sort or another, allowing me to draw on my experiences as a former sports writer. And all of them, I hope, still are written with the idea that I am producing an adult novel—for a young adult, to be sure, but still an adult.

I have a wife who is very supportive of my reclusive avocation and two married children, a son who has read every book I've written, and a daughter who, I think, has not read a one.

Bibliography

Books for Young Adults

1977   *Running Scared*
1978   *Winning Kicker*
1979   *Outside Shooter*
1980   *Point Spread*
1981   *Soccer Duel*
1982   *Quarterback Walk-On*
1983   *Rebound Caper*
1984   *Tournament Upstart*
1985   *Wilderness Peril*
1986   *Halfback Tough*

Jeannette Eyerly

From age ten, I was presumably responsible enough to take the streetcar and go downtown by myself to take my music lesson (in 1918 Des Moines was a medium-sized city of 130,000 or so). Each time upon my return, my mother would ask if I had had any "adventures."

My answer was always "yes," for if I had not actually had one, I always managed to magnify a small experience into something of epic proportions.

I am lucky that this ability to "invent" has stayed with me, as has the interest in practically everything that, as a child, made my trips home from "downtown" take so long.

Although I did not know it then, "inventing" and "loitering" were good practice for becoming an author, an ambition I'd cherished since I'd had a poem published in the Children's Corner of our evening newspaper two years before.

It was still my ambition when I graduated from the University of Iowa. Although it was at the bottom of the "Great Depression," I managed to get a job of sorts and save enough money for a two-month lark around Europe. Home again, I married my long-time sweetheart, Frank Eyerly, and went about fulfilling my writing ambition.

In those early days as a young wife and mother, with my second-hand typewriter on the kitchen table where I could dart from stove to sink to ironing board and still keep an eye on the children playing outdoors, I wore many hats. I was "Linda Lee" when I needed a light frothy viewpoint, and for more serious pieces I was "Miriam Carlock." When a male viewpoint was required I became "Sandy McTavish." For so-called "slick paper" magazines, I wrote assigned first-person stories on subjects of their choosing. For each I wore a different "hat."

63

Later on when my daughters, bored with what they called "teenage gum drops," suggested I write a book about "real kids with real problems," I discovered that simply from practice I already *was* a fiction writer.

In the turmoil of the sixties, subjects were not difficult to find. Letters from readers of *Drop Out; Escape from Nowhere; A Girl Like Me; Bonnie Jo, Go Home;* and others, required almost as much time to answer as it took to write the books that followed. Some of them were sad, a few were funny, but except for two suspense novels that I wrote to cheer myself up after writing *See Dave Run,* all had a "point." As a sampling: Don't drop out of school. Don't fool around with drugs. Don't make a baby until you are old enough and responsible enough to take care of it. Don't think for a minute that blind kids are any different than you are.

Although we don't have space for questions—always my favorite time when I visit your classrooms—I'm glad we have had this chance to become better acquainted. Should we never have this opportunity again, always remember when you read my books that you have a friend "out there."

Bibliography

Books for Young Adults

1962	*More Than a Summer Love*
1963	*Drop Out*
1964	*The World of Ellen March*
1966	*A Girl Like Me*
1966	*The Girl Inside*
1969	*Escape from Nowhere*
1970	*Radigan Cares*
1971	*The Phaedra Complex*
1972	*Bonnie Jo, Go Home*
1974	*Goodbye to Budapest: A Novel of Suspense*
1976	*The Leonardo Touch: A Novel of Suspense*
1977	*He's My Baby Now*
1978	*See Dave Run*
1980	*If I Loved You Wednesday*
1983	*Seth and Me and Rebel Make Three*
1984	*Angel Baker, Thief*
1987	*Someone to Love Me*

Books for Middle Graders

1965   *Gretchen's Hill*
1981   *The Seeing Summer*

Other Books

1961   *Dearest Kate* (with Valeria Winkler Griffith, under joint pseudonym Jeannette Griffith)
1988   *Writing Young Adult Novels* (with Hadley Irwin)

Paul Fleischman

I grew up ten blocks from the ocean in Santa Monica, California. Though my father, Sid Fleischman, was and is a writer, I didn't dream of seeing my own name in print. I'd no notion that our shortwave radio, our printing press, my bicycle, and the alto recorder would lead me toward writing as well.

The shortwave radio arrived when I was ten. Late at night, with the headphones on, I'd comb the dial in search of new stations. I didn't happen to speak Spanish or Chinese or Bulgarian or Arabic. Listening to a language you don't understand, you hear the sound of the words rather than their sense. Words, I discovered, have a music to them.

One day my parents came home with a hand printing press. I had my own printing business while I was in junior high school, printing stationery for my parents' friends. The shapes of letters and look of the words on a page, I found, are beautiful as well.

It was through my bicycle that I discovered history. My sisters and I loved to cruise Santa Monica's alleys, looking through people's trash. Nowadays I do much the same thing, as I did when researching Ohio farm life for *The Borning Room* or the lives of Civil War soldiers for *Bull Run;* I read old letters, skim through diaries, peeking into others' lives. At nineteen, I rode my bicycle and the train across the country to New Hampshire. There, I lived in a 200-year-old house, whose earlier occupants were buried in the tiny cemetery nearby. I could make out their names. I was living in their house, sleeping in the bedroom many of them had slept in. I felt a strong connection with them, with their times, and with New England, a connection that's led to many of my books.

I brought my alto recorder with me to New Hampshire and joined a consort. Playing music, I found, was much more fun than merely listening to it. And playing with others was far more exciting than playing alone. This revelation led, years later, to my two-voiced poems and to *Rondo in C* and *Bull Run* and several other books with multiple points of view.

I wanted to write music when I was younger. Then I wanted to teach history. I decided I wasn't qualified for either, but discovered that I could do both through writing books.

Bibliography

Books for Young Adults

1982	*Graven Images*
1983	*Path of the Pale Horse*
1985	*Coming-and-Going Men*
1985	*I Am Phoenix: Poems for Two Voices*
1986	*Rear-View Mirrors*
1988	*Joyful Noise: Poems for Two Voices*
1990	*Saturnalia*
1991	*The Borning Room*
1993	*Bull Run*

Books for Younger Readers

1979	*The Birthday Tree*
1980	*The Half-a-Moon Inn*
1983	*The Animal Hedge*
1983	*Phoebe Danger, Detective, in the Case of the Two-Minute Cough*
1983	*Finzel the Far-Sighted*
1988	*Rondo in C*
1990	*Shadow Play*
1991	*Time Train*
1992	*Townsend's Warbler*

Michael French

I was born into a middle-class family in Los Angeles after World War II, the youngest of two sons—a blond, blue-eyed surfer-to-be, but not without a certain purpose of character. I was influenced by my Methodist church, the discipline and idealism of my father (a medical doctor), and several good teachers along the way. As an adolescent, I felt a not untypical antagonism toward the world, and often I retreated to my typewriter. I could sit and compose for days on end. Romantic poetry and short stories with existential themes were my specialty. Of course, I sent everything I wrote immediately to *The New Yorker.* I was such a steady submitter that the editor sending back rejection notes came to address me as "Dear Michael." I pursued creative writing at Stanford University, where I graduated with a degree in English in 1966. A year later I earned my Master's in journalism from Northwestern University, my diploma coming exactly one day before I received another "Dear Michael"—from Uncle Sam.

I served two years as editor-in-chief of the Ft. Ord Fifth Army newspaper, in Monterey, California, which I found a superior place to be to Vietnam (I had an ocean view from my barracks, and no one shot at me), and which later formed the basis of my novel, *Soldier Boy.* After my liberation from uniforms and short haircuts, I married an extroverted New Yorker named Patricia Goodkind, moved to New York City, and took up writing as seriously as I knew how. I had my initial successes with adult fiction, but when my first young adult novel, *The Throwing Season,* was reviewed in *The New York Times,* I was so amazed that a critic had actually *read* my book, even liked it (mostly), I decided to write more for teenagers. I also fled New York for Santa Fe, New Mexico, where Patricia and I now live with our two teenagers, Timothy, age fifteen, and Alison, age thirteen.

I have an unintentional habit of writing books that either sell very well or not at all, good reviews and literary accomplishments notwithstanding. While this inconsistency often troubles my publishers, my focus on young adult fiction has always been on stories with meaningful themes and characters, as dark as they might be. I have never thought of writing as a popularity contest, though some people try to make it that. Judgment is generally unhealthy for the creative process; being left alone, buffered from pressures and distractions, is good. So is a second source of income (after teachers, writers are in the most underpaid profession in the universe). I've always been fascinated with the role of the idealist in a shaded world, and that subject plays an important theme in much of my fiction.

Bibliography

Books for Young Adults

1979   *The Throwing Season*
1981   *Pursuit*
1983   *Lifeguards Only Beyond This Point*
1985   *Us Against Them*
1986   *Soldier Boy*
1988   *Circle of Revenge*
1990   *Split Image*

Nancy Garden

PHOTO: © 1982 TIM MORSE

World War II was raging when I was little, and my dad was in the Red Cross. I was glad he was safe, but because of his job, we moved a lot, even after the war was over. It seemed to me that as soon as I got used to a new school and new friends, off we'd go again! Sometimes I was lonely, but because there were always books around, I couldn't stay lonely for long.

I started writing for my own pleasure when I was eight, and I went on writing no matter what else I did—when I was in theater, when I became a teacher (which I still am), when I had various office jobs, when I was an editor. One of the greatest things about writing is that you can do it just about anywhere—and one of the great things about being a writer who's had lots of different jobs is that the jobs, along with everything else one experiences, can provide material for stories.

I like reading different kinds of books, and I like writing different kinds of books, too. Nonfiction and historical fiction allow me to do research, which I've found is a terrific way to learn new things. I like writing mysteries because I like making up puzzles, and I like horror and fantasy because I believe anything is possible, even the improbable. Most of all, though, I like writing serious fiction, for I know that growing up isn't always easy, and I believe kids can help make the world a better place; kids in my books often do. My book, *Peace, O River,* is about a girl who tries to solve a conflict between two towns and two groups of kids; in my mind, at least, it's also about war and peace on a wider scale. *What Happened in Marston* deals with race relations, and *Annie on My Mind* is about the right of two people of the same sex to love each other.

When I talk to people about writing, some of them ask me what they should do if they want to be writers. My answer is

70

READ, WRITE, and REVISE—I guess you could call those the three Rs of writing. READING (besides being fun) is a great way to find out about literary styles and the way other writers create characters and plots. (It's also, if you're alert, a pretty painless way to learn grammar, spelling, and punctuation.) WRITING, of course, is vital practice; a writer can get rusty just as an athlete can. It's important to try to write something every day, your diary, a letter, a book review. And then it's important to REVISE. This is what beginners tend to skimp on, but most professional writers rewrite many, many times. One thing revising shows you is that there are usually many ways to say the same thing.

Your job as a writer is to find the best one you can!

Bibliography

Books for Young Adults

1972   *The Loners*
1972   *Berlin: City Split in Two* (nonfiction)
1982   *Annie on My Mind*
1986   *Peace, O River*
1991   *Lark in the Morning*

Books for Middle Graders

1972   *What Happened in Marston*
1973   *Vampires* (nonfiction)
1973   *Werewolves* (nonfiction)
1975   *Witches* (nonfiction)
1976   *Devils and Demons* (nonfiction)
1992   *My Sister the Vampire*

The Fours Crossing Series

1981   *Fours Crossing*
1983   *Watersmeet*
1987   *The Door Between*

Monster Hunters Series

1987   *Case #1: Mystery of the Night Raiders*
1988   *Case #2: Mystery of the Midnight Menace*
1989   *Case #3: Mystery of the Secret Marks*
1992   *Case #4: Mystery of the Kidnapped Kidnapper*

Books for Younger Readers

1977	*Fun With Weather Forecasting* (nonfiction)
1981	*Maria's Mountain*
1982	*Favorite Tales from Grimm*
1991	*The Kid's Code and Cipher Book* (nonfiction)

Leon Garfield

I was born in Brighton at the age of ten days. Hence, at some time in my early life, I must have astonished onlookers by being able to perform feats of intellectual skill a full ten days in advance of my fellows. But, alas, I was no prodigy. My father, a gentleman of feckless charm, had neglected to register my birth, and, taking fright that he might have to pay a fine, set me down as having been born on July the twenty-fourth, instead of July the fourteenth. From this confusion, I have never really recovered.

When I was little, I was mercifully spared the advantages that seem to have befriended other writers. Neither my mother nor my father told me stories (other than where I came from); I had no garrulous grandmother to tell me tales of old St. Petersburg, Vienna, Baghdad, Warsaw, or Budapest. Nor did I own an aged retainer who filled my young mind with her lunatic babblings. Instead, my earliest acquaintance with the romance of life was gained by eavesdropping and hearing of my father's numerous strayings and the calamitous exploits of a gloriously unsuccessful uncle who was the toast of all the cafés and boulevards of Brighton.

I had another uncle (I seem to have had dozens!), a scowling, shouting fellow, married to a sour little pudding of a virtuous aunt. They lived in a tall dark house in North London, inhabited by funereal furniture, camphor balls, and Lithuanian rabbis, who seemed to lurk behind every plum-coloured velvet curtain, like Polonius in the play. I was sent there on holidays, as a punishment, I suppose. Certainly, it gave me powerful ideas of sin. To this day, I conceive of hell as being presided over by that uncle and aunt, who used to bring home live carp wrapped in wet newspaper and keep them in a tin bath in the kitchen before knocking them on the head, disembowelling them, and serving them up for supper.

So I began writing stories; mostly, I think, they were wish-fulfilment stories, of vengeful phantoms laying waste to Highbury New Park (where my aunt and uncle lived), and ghastly Egyptian mummies (all of whom bore a striking resemblance to my aunt) with poison behind their eyes.

I liked writing stories. It was the only thing for which I showed the smallest aptitude. In every other branch of human activity, I was a nonstarter. I remember, it was many years before I grasped the notion that logarithms were a mathematical concept and not a species of venomous reptile found in Venezuela.

But my stories prospered. I was a great imitator. I dredged the classics (if you're going to steal, steal from the best!) and embroidered my work with their pearls. Looking back now on the various stages through which I passed, I shudder with horror. But some people seemed to discern some glimmerings of gold among the dross, notably an English teacher, by name of Mr. Randall, and, much later, Vivien Alcock, my wife.

I met her in Belgium, during the war, and fell in love with her instantly. How could I have failed to? She was interested in what I wrote. I wrote incessantly, short stories and at least three novels of gruesome incompetence. Then, at last, I hit upon an idea that really was an idea for a novel, and not an anecdote to be stretched on a rack. It was a tale of ships and pirates, of tropical forests, and a trial at the Old Bailey—a trial such as never was! It took me five years to write. When I'd finished, I submitted it to an agent and awaited, with the gloom of long experience, its unhappy return. But, to my astonishment, and, I think, to my wife's, there proved to be a publisher foolhardy enough to publish it. Her name was Grace Hogarth, and, next to my wife, I think she is the most wonderful person I have every known. She published *Jack Holborn!* To my profound relief, her courage was rewarded. The book was well-received, none of my thievings were detected, and hope was expressed for my future.

Since then, I have gone from success to excess, and back again. But laurels are uncomfortable things to sit back upon; so I toil away, always nervous for Vivien's good opinion, and always feeling that I am still learning how to write.

Bibliography

1964   *Jack Holborn*
1966   *Devil-in-the-Fog*
1967   *Smith*
1968   *Black Jack*
1969   *Mister Corbett's Ghost and Other Stories*
1969   *The Boy and the Monkey*
1970   *The Drummer Boy*
1970   *The God Beneath the Sea* (with Edward Blishen)
1971   *The Strange Affair of Adelaide Harris*
1972   *The Ghost Downstairs*
1972   *The Captain's Watch*
1972   *Child O' War* (with David Proctor)
1973   *Lucifer Wilkins*
1973   *Baker's Dozen*
1973   *The Golden Shadow* (with Edward Blishen)
1974   *The Sound of Coaches*
1975   *The Prisoners of September*
1976   *The Pleasure Garden*
1976   *The Booklovers*
1976   *The House of Hanover*
1976   *The Lamplighter's Funeral*
1976   *Mirror, Mirror*
1976   *Moss and Blister*
1976   *The Cloak*
1977   *The Valentine*
1977   *Labour in Vain*
1977   *The Fool*
1977   *The Dumb Cake*
1977   *Tom Titmarsh's Devil*
1977   *The Filthy Beast*
1977   *The Enemy*
1978   *The Confidence Man*
1978   *Bostock & Harris*
1980   *John Diamond*
1980   *Mystery of Edwin Drood*
1981   *Fair's Fair*
1982   *The House of Cards*
1982   *King Nimrod's Tower*
1982   *The Apprentices*
1983   *The Writing on the Wall*

Patricia Lee Gauch

PHOTO: © JON ROEMER

I was born in Detroit, Michigan, near Lake St. Clair. Indeed, I lived so close to the lake, I could hear the freighter horns at night. The long boats moved across the horizon like great monsters, and I wondered where they went and where they had come from. I wished that I could ride one to discover those secrets.

Wishing, dreaming, was clearly a part of my childhood. The only child of youngish parents, Melbourne and Muriel Lee, without brothers and sisters, I had plenty of time to dream, to play "make believe": prince and princess, soldiers, "house." Whether outside with the other children on my block—there were seventy-six under fifteen years of age at one time—or at home alone, I lived in wonder-filled worlds.

However, dreaming is not writing. Unlike some children, I did not elect to be a writer at the age of ten. I didn't know what I wanted to be, but I had an uncle, Ray Pearson, who was a crusty city editor at the *Detroit Free Press*. Sometimes he would have an article on the front page—with his name on it! Joy! And at the Sunday dinner tables, we would hear about the adventures that he had discovering the story of an embezzler or a bigamist.

It seemed impossible to me to be a reporter on a daily newspaper, but then I attended Miami University in Oxford, Ohio, where I had the grand opportunity of being a reporter and finally editor-in-chief of the college newspaper, *The Miami Student*. Now I could track down all kinds of stories (including the ghost in Fisher Hall) and I could have my byline on the front page.

I never did feel that I picked writing as a career; somehow, I felt that writing picked me. I married Ron Gauch before I graduated, a brave thing to do in those days; I was only twenty-one. And when he went to Fort Knox, I went along and talked myself into a job as a reporter on the *Louisville Courier Journal*. At twenty-three I was interviewing the likes of historian Alfred Toynbee and movie star Robert Q. Lewis and loving the adventure of it.

In the 1950s there was considerable difficulty breaking into the news side of journalism, and my having children and returning to Detroit—and newspapers there that hired mostly males—forced me to think about what other kinds of writing I might like to do. Since I was still a reporter at heart—curious (nosy is the truth of it), interested in tracking down mysteries—I took a good look at historical writing. Indeed, I fell in love with the flamboyant French and Indian War major Robert Rogers and, without knowing what I would do with my research, I began to study him. (That study took me to cemeteries in New Hampshire, archives in Ann Arbor, a fort in Michigan!)

As a child I had always been a reader. I read every picture book on the shelves, and the Laura Ingalls Wilder books. I read *Anne of Green Gables* and other Montgomery books. At about the same time I discovered boys, I discovered *Seventeenth Summer* and loved it. But discovering nonfiction and historical fiction was a particular pleasure. How I loved biographies.

My first book then, not surprisingly, was a biography of Rogers. It didn't sell, but writing it introduced me to a woman who was a member of the Jean Fritz Writer's Workshop in Katonah, New York, where Ron and I had recently moved. I joined the workshop, a fortuitous joining since so many years later I would use the critiquing I learned in those lively, boisterous sessions in my position as editor in chief at Philomel Books.

As a wife and mother, I had unusual freedom to study and write. I returned to school twice, once to get a teaching degree (MAT) from Manhattanville College, and later a doctorate in English literature from Drew University. During this same time, I have raised three children, have taught, and have written more than twenty-five books. Like many authors, I have frequently written for the age my children were at the time: picture books, middle fiction, novels.

I believe it is no mistake that I ventured out. To be a writer, I think one must. By observing (really observing), by living, we create a rich reservoir of character and story; from it, we draw the themes of our lives that will play themselves out over and over in our books.

In mine, not surprisingly, it is the strong female heroine, who is not so big and strong, but resilient: Christina in the *Christina* books, Corey in *Fridays*, Jennifer in *The Green of Me*, Tillie in *Thunder at*

Gettysburg, sturdy female characters who are creative, idealistic, even invincible, and who seek and meet adventure with courage and a good, healthy sense of humor. I hope that it is my story as well.

Bibliography

Books for Young Adults

1978	*The Green of Me*
1979	*Fridays*
1980	*Kate Alone*
1981	*Morelli's Game*
1983	*Night Talk*
1985	*The Year the Summer Died*

Books for Younger Readers

1972	*Aaron and the Green Mountain Boys*
1974	*This Time, Tempe Wick?* (reissued 1992)
1975	*Thunder at Gettysburg* (reissued 1991)
1977	*The Impossible Major Rogers*

Picture Books

1970	*My Old Tree*
1972	*Grandpa and Me*
1972	*Christina Katerina and the Box*
1973	*A Secret House*
1973	*Christina Katerina and the First Annual Grand Ballet*
1976	*The Little Friar that Flew*
1977	*Once Upon a Dinkelsbuhl*
1978	*On to Widecombe Fair*
1987	*Christina Katerina and the Time She Quit the Family*
1990	*Christina Katerina and the Great Bear Train*
1990	*Dance, Tanya*
1992	*Bravo, Tanya*
1992	*Uncle Magic*

Jan Greenberg

I grew up on a tree-lined street in suburban St. Louis in a duplex that my parents shared with my aunt, uncle, and cousins. It was one big not-so-happy family, filled with intrigue, rivalries, laughter, and tears. Wonderful material to draw upon for fiction. Since both my parents worked, I was sent to a private girl's school—the only place in town that had an all-day program for three-year-olds. There I stayed for fourteen years until I graduated and went away to college. That very conservative but rigorous school with its many rules and traditions became the setting of my first novel, *A Season In-Between*.

My mother was an advertising executive at a big department store. I spent many hours of my childhood in her office learning to draw from the layout artists and listening to sessions on ad campaigns. My appreciation for visual images, as well as the power of language, resulted from that experience. When I was about ten, I contracted a strange eye allergy. My eyes watered every time I went outside. Most of that summer, I stayed inside, poring over all the books in my parents' library. There I developed a strong love of reading, as well as a notion of myself as an outsider. This feeling comes through in many of my novels. Although I didn't know it then, I know now that all of us have a strain of insecurity, which runs deep inside us. This may be the reason that realistic fiction about young people with problems is so popular.

To counter that image of myself, I became the class cut-up. Since my novels are based on my own life, I don't write about tidy, perfect children who behave like the Brady Bunch. My characters fall more into the Dennis the Menace category. Many people have asked me what kind of a miserable childhood did I have to invent such cranky, persnickety kids who say things like, "I feel like the only matzaball in a bowl of chicken dumpling soup." But the truth is, my childhood wasn't unusually miserable at all. Yes, I had eye allergies and boy troubles. I was too tall; I thought my parents were too strict, my teachers unfair . . . but then these complaints and a host of new ones cropped up in regular cycles with my own daughters as well. Perhaps this is the reason I started writing about teenagers in the first place.

Yet, always the eternal optimist, I believe in finding some kind of resolution to these problems. I'd rather have my characters walk out of a hurricane than into one at the end of a novel.

My college career was uneventful, except for the fact that, given some independence, I proceeded to have a wonderful time. I did write a winning short story based on a humorous episode from my dubious high school career. This small recognition encouraged me to continue writing and exploring autobiographical material.

For many years, I was an art educator working with teachers, artists, and actors. After my first novel was published in 1979, I began to write full-time, although I still visited classrooms and gave writing workshops. My husband opened a contemporary art gallery in St. Louis in 1971. The gallery and our old rambling house became a center for visiting artists, curators, and collectors. These friendships and my interest in "new" art forms prompted me to write *The Painter's Eye: Learning to Look at Contemporary American Art.* I began with a question: What do you say after you say I like it or don't like it? When I start a novel, I also make lists of questions that begin "What if. . . ." Questions are open-ended and filled with possibilities. So are the answers.

If I could give any advice to those of you who want to be writers I would say, be curious and open to new ideas. Let your imagination run free. Don't worry about writing the perfect sentence or you'll never get past the first line. You can always edit later.

Bibliography

Books for Young Adults and Middle Graders
1979   *A Season In-Between*
1980   *The Iceberg and Its Shadow*
1982   *The Pig-Out Blues*
1983   *No Dragons to Slay*
1985   *Bye, Bye Miss American Pie*
1986   *Exercises of the Heart*

Patricia Hermes

When I was a child, the voice I heard at twilight was the voice of the storyteller. Sometimes the storyteller was my mother, sometimes my father or an older sibling—but always, at bedtime, I could count on the storyteller. And from my first awareness of those twilight storytimes, even long before I could read for myself, I knew that someday I, too, would be a storyteller.

I was born February 21, 1936, the third of four children, and I grew up feeling very much a MIDDLE child. And I HATED that! Even physically, I felt very "middle." I was neither too tall nor too small. My hair was straight, neither blonde nor brown, but some boring shade in between. Intellectually, too, I felt ordinary and "middle." I wasn't a genius, but I knew I wasn't dumb, either.

I was, however, smart enough to know that all around me a world was going on, a child's world full of play and mischief and an adult world full of intrigue and mystery, one from which we children were shut out. I was also smart enough to understand that if I was to be a storyteller, the way to learn, to collect material for my stories, was to keep quiet. To listen. To watch.

And to record it all.

These are some of the things I discovered as I listened, watched, and recorded this world around me. I learned that pets—and people—die. I learned that sometimes bad things happened to children, things we children couldn't control. I learned that nights were scary because there really ARE monsters in the dark. I learned that siblings could be a pain, but also most loveable. I knew that people who smiled were not necessarily nice, and that sometimes—not often, but occasionally—those who were grouchy were actually solid and fine beneath their grumps.

These are just some of the things I learned as a child, some of the things I write about today.

I did not immediately begin writing when I grew up, however, at least, not professional writing. Instead, I became a teacher, and then spent many years being a full-time mother. Then, around 1980, I again turned to writing and storytelling, seriously, professionally. I have written books about kids who are ill because I had some lengthy illnesses as a child. I write frequently about "only" children, thereby getting rid of my unnecessary siblings. I have written one book, *Mama, Let's Dance*, that contains much about myself as a child and my relationship with my baby sister.

I also write about real children, my own children today. I do not consciously set out to write about my children, but they seem to creep into my stories, and it's only afterwards that I realize they are there. In my book, *You Shouldn't Have to Say Goodbye*, the girl Sarah is definitely my own daughter, Jennifer. In the book, *I Hate Being Gifted*, all five children are very much like my own four sons and daughter. In my books, *Kevin Corbett Eats Flies* and *Heads, I Win*, the character of the little brother, Matthew, is a lot like my own son, Matthew. And so forth. . . .

It's important to remember, however, that all of what I write is fiction, that is, the stories are just that—stories—and not true accounts of my life. Yet each story, in some way, has some small grain of experience or of feeling from which it springs, something that IS my truth.

Today, I travel frequently, speaking to adults and young people all over the country. I love traveling and speaking, and love especially the children that I meet. But when I return home and turn to my writing, I feel the same thrill and joy that I felt long ago during those twilight story hours. Home at my desk, with my paper and pen, I become once again the storyteller that I always knew I would be, setting down for others the stories I recorded early, the stories that are in my heart.

Bibliography

Books for Young Adults

1984	*Friends Are Like That*
1985	*A Solitary Secret*
1987	*A Time to Listen*
1989	*Be Still My Heart*

Books for Younger Readers

1980	*What If They Knew*
1981	*Nobody's Fault*
1982	*Who Will Take Care of Me?*
1983	*You Shouldn't Have to Say Good-bye*
1984	*Friends Are Like That*
1986	*Kevin Corbett Eats Flies*
1987	*A Place for Jeremy*
1988	*Heads, I Win*
1990	*I Hate Being Gifted*
1991	*Mama, Let's Dance*
1991	*My Girl* (novelization of screenplay)
1992	*Take Care of My Girl*

Jamake Highwater

PHOTO: HENRY KURTH

Because I was adopted and my adoptive parents were unusually secretive about their pasts, I have never known for certain where or when I was born. The first eight years or so of my life are made up of inexact recollections and often contradictory information.

My mother, I have learned, was a blend of French Canadian and Blackfeet (Blood) ancestry. My father was likely of Eastern Cherokee heritage, though I am uncertain of his parentage. I do recall that he was a renegade and an alcoholic who called himself by many names during his careers in circuses, wild west shows, rodeos, and motion pictures as a stuntman. My mother, though she could neither read nor write, was a marvelous storyteller. From her, I learned to stay alive by dreaming myself into existence. I learned that *everything* is real. That idea has been the most important lesson in my life as a creative artist and as an individual.

Acquaintances of my father in the movie industry took me in as if I were a stray dog. My foster mother came to love me, but my foster father had no use for me. At one point, I was placed in an orphanage where I spent two or three lonely and painful years. After my father's death, my foster parents adopted me and I was raised in the San Fernando Valley of southern California in a household of many secrets. Although my mother approved of me, she took no interest in my work, nor did she encourage me or read anything I wrote. For many years, the youngest of my foster sisters was the single most important person in my life. I shared with her all the love I did not share with my parents.

This profile has been compiled and edited from previously published autobiographical pieces. Copyright: The Native Land Foundation.

In elementary school I did poorly until I encountered a social studies teacher named Alta Black who made me feel as if she cared about me. The effort to please her gave me the motivation to become one of the most accomplished students in the school. And it was she who gave me an old Royal portable typewriter and told me she had dreamed that I was going to be a writer.

I started to write a succession of rambling novels and short stories, sharing them only with my mentors, James Leo Herlihy and Anaïs Nin. In high school and college, I studied creative writing, organized film programs, staged musicals and class plays, and directed amateur radio productions. In 1954 I resettled in San Francisco and got a job teaching dance, while continuing to write on the side. Eventually, I founded the San Francisco Contemporary Theatre company with several refugees from the tap-dancing school, and we toured the country throughout the 1960s, before I decided to move to New York City and start all over as a writer.

In California, my gifts as an artist had always been regarded as risky or useless, but in New York I was no longer perceived as eccentric. I discovered that great art exists as I do, without an apparent history. Perhaps it is the very fact that art seems to arise out of nothing that makes both art and the artist timeless. In the early 1970s, I was introduced to the young adult market when I wrote *Anpao*. It won the Newbery Honor Award as well as the Boston Globe/Horn Book Honor Award. I did not intend that novel to be for young people, but I consider myself fortunate to have found it possible to cross that great barrier that people normally construct between writing for children and writing for adults. I cherish young readers as readers, not as children.

Living in New York and in Europe in the early '70s, I finally had made a name for myself. But it wasn't my own. As a child I was variously called "Jake," "Jay," "Jack," "John," and "Corky," but was known for many years as J Marks (with no period after the J). In the middle of my success, I legally changed my name to its preadoptive form: Jamake Highwater. It is who I am. And this is my story. But if people want to find out who I really am, they will find me in my work.

Bibliography

Novels
1977   *Anpao: An American Indian Odyssey*
1978   *Journey to the Sky*

1978	*The Sun, He Dies*
1986	*Eyes of Darkness*
1992	*Kill Hole*
1993	*Dark Legend*

The Ghost Horse Cycle

1984	*Legend Days*
1985	*The Ceremony of Innocence*
1986	*I Wear the Morning Star*

Nonfiction

1968	*Rock and Other Four Letter Words: Music of the Electric Generation* (under J Marks)
1973	*Mick Jagger: The Singer Not the Song* (under J Marks)
1975	*Fodor's Indian America*
1976	*Song from the Earth: Native American Painting*
1976	*Ritual of the Wind: Indian Ceremonies, Music, and Dances*
1978	*Many Smokes, Many Moons: A Chronology of American Indian History through Indian Art*
1978	*Dance: Rituals of Experience*
1980	*The Sweet Grass Lives On: Fifty Contemporary Indian Artists*
1981	*The Primal Mind: Vision and Reality in Indian America*
1983	*Leaves from the Sacred Tree: Arts of the Indian Americas*
1986	*Native Land: Sagas of American Civilizations*
1986	*Shadow Show: An Autobiographical Insinuation*
1988	*Athletes of the Gods: The Ritual Life of Sports*
1989	*Myth and Sexuality*
1992	*The World of 1492: The Americas*

Television Scripts

1977	*Songs of the Thunderbird*
1985	*The Primal Mind*
1986	*Native Land*

Poetry

1985	*Moonsong Lullaby*
1993	*Songs for the Seasons*

Edited Works

1972	*Fodor's Europe Under 25: The Young Person's Guide* (under J Marks-Highwater, with Eugene Fodor)
1984	*Words in the Blood: Contemporary Indian Writers of North and South America*

Douglas Hill

I was born in a town called Brandon in the province of Manitoba, Canada, and grew up in a town called Prince Albert in the neighbouring province, Saskatchewan. (Pause while you check your atlas.) And I'm still a Canadian today, in nationality and accent, though I've lived for more than thirty years in London, England.

I've also been a professional writer for nearly all of those thirty years. For the last fifteen years or so, I've mostly been writing science fiction and fantasy for younger readers.

Those are just about the only interesting facts there are about me. But I find that those facts about myself often make people ask—how come? So I'll tell you.

How come I live in England? Because I'd had a driving ambition to be a writer from about the age of ten. Because I got to the stage of wanting to see if I could make it in the "big leagues," which, for a would-be writer in the English language, back then, meant New York or London. So when I left university I came to look at London. And, as things turned out, I stayed.

How come I write science fiction and fantasy for young people? Because I've been addicted to those things, as a reader, for most of my life. At first, though, I wrote other things, everything from poetry to journalism, all nonfiction. But I became a reviewer of science fiction, an advisor to publishers, and other things. And I became convinced that there should be more SF and fantasy produced for young people, who are the most natural readership, with their imaginations at their most fully active.

One day I said as much to a remarkable young publisher's editor. She nodded calmly and said, "Have *you* ever thought of writing SF for kids?" And a big bright light went on inside my head, as in cartoons.

It's still on, as bright as ever, a great many books later.

For any young person reading this who has some ambition to be a writer, there's an important fact in the foregoing, though it's not just about me. The fact is that almost no one has become a successful writer of imaginative fiction (SF, fantasy, horror, all that) without first being a *reader* of it. Usually an addict. The reading, over the years, tunes and programmes the imagination. It's the only possible training and preparation for that kind of writing.

So if you're an avid reader of science fiction and fantasy—and if you also like writing stories—there's a pretty good chance that one day you might be earning your living the same way I do.

Which means you'll be feeling as lucky as I've felt, and having as much fun as I've had, ever since that light went on in my head.

Bibliography

Books for Young Adults

1975   *Coyote the Trickster* (with Gail Robinson)
1978   *Exploits of Hercules*
1979   *Galactic Warlord*
1980   *Deathwing Over Veynaa*
1980   *Day of the Starwind*
1982   *Planet of the Warlord*
1982   *Young Legionary*
1982   *The Huntsman*
1983   *Have Your Own Extraterrestrial Adventure*
1983   *Warriors of the Wasteland*
1984   *Alien Citadel*
1984   *Exiles of Colsec*
1984   *The Caves of Klydor*
1985   *Colsec Rebellion*
1985   *The Last Legionary Quartet* (omnibus edition)
1987   *Blade of the Poisoner*
1987   *Master of Fiends*

Books for Younger Readers

1984   *Moon Monsters*
1986   *How Jennifer (and Speckle) Saved the Earth*
1988   *Goblin Party*
1990   *Penelope's Pendant*

| 1990 | *The Tale of Trellie the Troog* |
| 1991 | *The Unicorn Dream* |

Fiction Books for Adults

1989	*The Fraxilly Fracas*
1990	*The Colloghi Conspiracy*
1992	*The Lightless Dome*

Nonfiction Books for Adults

1965	*The Supernatural* (with Pat Williams)
1966	*The Peasants' Revolt*
1967	*The Opening of the Canadian West*
1968	*Magic and Superstition*
1969	*Regency London*
1969	*John Keats*
1970	*100 Years of Georgian London*
1971	*Fortune Telling*
1971	*Bridging a Continent* (as Martin Hillman)
1971	*Return from the Dead*
1972	*The Scots to Canada*
1973	*The Comet*
1975	*The English to New England*
1978	*Fortune Telling: A Guide . . .*
1978	*The Illustrated "Faerie Queene"*

Edited Anthologies for Adults

1966	*Window on the Future*
1966	*Way of the Werewolf*
1967	*The Devil His Due*
1971	*Warlocks and Warriors*
1977	*Tribune 40*
1978	*The Shape of Sex to Come*

Edited Anthologies for Younger Readers

| 1981 | *Alien Worlds* |
| 1986 | *Planetfall* |

Will Hobbs

Every three years or so, we were off to somewhere new. We were an Air Force family; I have three brothers and a sister. The hard part was leaving friends behind, the good part was that we developed a sense of adventure about life and drew close to each other. I was born in Pittsburgh, Pennsylvania, in 1947, and grew up in the Panama Canal Zone, in Virginia, Alaska, California, and Texas. No matter where we lived, I was a reader, so I found school enjoyable. We didn't write fiction in school in those days, but early on I began to nurture the little flame of a dream that one day I would write stories myself.

I completed my bachelor's and master's in English at Stanford University. Living in California, I was able to spend a lot of time hiking and camping in the Sierras. In early college, I worked as a guide at Philmont Scout Ranch in northern New Mexico, and first discovered the Southwest. These mountains and canyons have been my home since 1972, when I moved to Colorado.

I was asked recently if I'm more a romantic, an idealist, or a pragmatist. The pragmatist in me isn't dominant; after all, I was an English major. I'll readily confess to being both a romantic and an idealist. I came of age in the early '60s—I was a junior in high school when I stood on the curb in San Antonio, Texas, on November 21, 1963, and watched President Kennedy pass within a few feet along the parade route. The idealism and sense of social responsibility of that era is something I hope to bring to my writing.

I taught English and reading in high school and junior high for seventeen years. What I liked best was matching kids with books. My sense of audience comes from thousands of one-on-one conferences with students, discussing books they had just finished reading. In 1980, I started my own novel. *Bearstone* is set in the back country of the Weminuche Wilderness, very close to home. The places in the novel are real and I visit them often. Nephews and nieces come to us for "summer camp," and we take them out hiking in the back country.

Changes in Latitudes, my first published novel, is about the intermingled fates of endangered sea turtles and an endangered American family vacationing in Mexico. The seed for this story was the joy I felt as a small child holding a box turtle in my hand, along with an image I had of what it would be like to swim with sea turtles.

My wife Jean and I have been running rivers since about 1977. Our favorite is the Grand Canyon, an eighteen-day whitewater rafting trip. Recently, on our seventh trip, we ran it, just the two of us. In my novel *Downriver,* along with telling a story of personal growth and responsibility, I wanted to bring the excitement and the beauty of the canyon to life for readers. I hope *Downriver* will get them wet!

The Big Wander takes readers to some of the most remote canyon country in the Southwest. It's a romantic adventure, one that is meant to inspire in readers the affection I've felt for wild places and the other creatures with whom we share the planet. I can't help but think that if young people love the natural world, they'll want to help preserve it.

Bibliography

Books for Young Adults
1988   *Changes in Latitudes*
1989   *Bearstone*
1991   *Downriver*
1992   *The Big Wander*

Felice Holman

I grew up on Long Island, New York, in a family that valued creativity. My mother was an artist and a singer. My father loved music, and the radio was tuned to the symphony every Saturday and to the opera every Sunday. Since my father was deaf in one ear, due to a bicycle accident in his youth, the decibels of the music were overwhelming and caused me to retreat to my room where, today, they might say that I "did my own thing" but, then, they said that I "moped." However, while I moped, I wrote.

I always knew I would be a writer. My Aunt Marie was a psychic and she believed in Hindu theories of immortality. She told me I was the reincarnation of a famous woman writer. I started writing poetry very early, and the first book, at about age eight, was a one-volume edition of poetry, handwritten by me, and illustrated in pastels by my mother.

When I was going to college, the effects of the Great Depression were still about, and my father suggested it might be wise to learn to become something that would earn me a living—like a hotel manager. I'm not too good at managing things, so I studied journalism and thought I'd be a newspaper reporter. At the first class, the dean of the School of Journalism said, "Look at the person seated at your right and look at the person seated on your left: one of those people is not going to be a journalist." It turned out it wasn't the person on my right or left, but me. I could write, but I wasn't enterprising or gregarious enough to make a good reporter. It seems there's more to being a good journalist than being able to write.

To earn a living for a while, I wrote advertising copy in New York City. I turned out to be very good at it and won a lot of prizes for good ideas, but I never got over the feeling that I was helping sell people a lot of stuff they really didn't need. So I was very happy when I was able to spend my time living in Connecticut, taking care of my family, and writing things I wanted to write. What I wanted to write was poetry and books for young people. And, years later, that's what I'm still doing. So my aunt may have been right!

I love what I do and I don't want to stop. I'm getting old as the oceans—I was born October 24, 1919—but I am just starting a new form of writing (new for me): I'm living in California and learning to write screenplays. When you're a writer, it doesn't matter much how old you are, as long as your mind spins and your fingers fly.

The last several years I have been writing about things that concern me deeply: stories about survival (*Slake's Limbo*); about children alone (*The Wild Children*); and my most recent novel about street children who help themselves (*Secret City, U.S.A.*). I want to communicate my thoughts to young people because I believe in their potential. I believe that with motivation, and good direction, and a little help, they can grow up to do something to make things better . . . for themselves and for everyone.

Bibliography

Books for Young Adults

1974	*Slake's Limbo*
1978	*The Murderer*
1983	*The Wild Children*
1990	*Secret City, U.S.A.*

Books for Middle Graders

1960	*The Holiday Rat and the Utmost Mouse*
1965	*Professor Diggins' Dragons*
1966	*The Witch on the Corner*
1967	*The Cricket Winter*
1968	*A Year to Grow*
1968	*The Blackmail Machine*
1970	*At the Top of My Voice and Other Poems*
1972	*The Future of Hooper Toote*
1973	*I Hear You Smiling and Other Poems*

1974	*The Escape of the Giant Hogstalk*
1975	*The Drac: French Tales of Dragons and Demons* (with Nanine Valen)
1985	*The Song in My Head* (poems)

Books for Younger Readers

1962	*Elisabeth the Birdwatcher*
1964	*Elisabeth the Treasure Hunter*
1965	*Silently the Cat and Miss Theodosia*
1966	*Elisabeth and the Marsh Mystery*
1966	*Victoria's Castle*
1970	*Solomon's Search*
1987	*Terrible Jane*

Monica Hughes

PHOTO: RUSS HUGHES

I was born in 1925, in Liverpool, England, but moved with my parents to live in Cairo, Egypt, for the next five years. On our return to England my younger sister and I went to a wonderful girls' school in a London suburb, where myths, legends, and the Norse sagas were read aloud to us. I discovered the world of magic in the stories of E. Nesbit, and, when we moved to Edinburgh, Scotland, I found the exciting works of the nineteenth-century adventure writers. I told stories to my younger sister and began to dream of being a writer myself.

During the Second World War I was in the Women's Royal Naval Service and afterwards lived in Zimbabwe, working in a dress factory and a bank before coming to Canada in 1952, where I worked at the National Research Council in Ottawa. All through these years I wrote short stories and novels, but received only rejection slips.

I was married in 1957, and in 1964 moved to Edmonton, Alberta, with my husband Glen and our four children, Elizabeth, Adrienne, Russell, and Thomas. In 1971, with the children in school, I decided to try writing *full-time*. I discovered the terrific juvenile novels that had been written in the 1950s and '60s and knew I wanted to become a writer for young people. I had found my voice.

I wrote for four hours a day at the kitchen table, with a black Bic pen on looseleaf paper, painfully typing it later. I still use the same system, only now I have a word processor to help me edit. The third book I wrote, *Crisis on Conshelf Ten,* was accepted by an international publisher in 1974. Since that day, I have had twenty-five books published, with two more on the way, plus a number of short stories.

97

What turned a lifetime of rejection slips into success? Partly perseverance. I also learned that ideas are everywhere and it is important to recognize them and to *write them down*. I have an "ideas" file full of newspaper clippings of scientific facts and human interest stories—such as the current unemployment of young people in North Britain, which was the "starter" for *Invitation to the Game*. I am particularly interested in the tension between scientific progress and the health of our environment, so a lot of cuttings and ideas on this goes into my file. I learned how to use my right imaginative brain *and* my logical left brain together. I learned, too, how to use the library for research, especially for science fiction books, so as to have a setting that is truly believable, and how to develop characters by thinking about them and their life *before* page one.

I swim, garden, and enjoy Taoist Tai Chi and traveling. I love difficult crosswords, jigsaws, and mathematical puzzles. I enjoy socializing with my family and friends, especially other writers, and am involved in local church activities.

Bibliography

Books for Young Adults

1974   *Gold-Fever Trail*
1975   *Crisis on Conshelf Ten*
1977   *Earthdark*
1978   *The Tomorrow City*
1978   *Ghost Dance Caper*
1979   *Beyond the Dark River*
1980   *The Keeper of the Isis Light*
1981   *The Guardian of Isis*
1982   *The Isis Pedlar*
1982   *Hunter in the Dark*
1982   *Ring-Rise, Ring-Set*
1982   *The Beckoning Lights*
1982   *The Treasure of the Long Sault*
1983   *Space Trap*
1983   *My Name Is Paula Popowich!*
1984   *Devil on My Back*
1985   *Sandwriter*
1986   *The Dream Catcher*
1986   *Blaine's Way*
1987   *Log Jam*

1988	*Spirit River*
1989	*The Promise*
1989	*The Refuge*
1990	*Invitation to the Game*
1992	*The Crystal Drop*

Picture Books

| 1989 | *Little Fingerling* |

Mollie Hunter

he'll go her own way in spite of fate!" This, from my birth in 1922 onwards, was my mother's repeated comment about me. And she was right!

Mine was a village childhood in southeast Scotland; a happy one, too, until my father died, leaving five young children behind him. With no money then for higher education, we all had to leave school at fourteen to try to earn our keep. But I was already determined to be a writer, and I'd had teachers who helped and encouraged me in this.

Every spare hour I had, I studied; and it was from the two subjects that intrigued me most—folklore and Scottish history—that I was later to cull material for a long line of fantasy and historical adventure novels. All of these, however, were written post-World War II, by which time I had married and settled down in the place where I still live—a beautiful glen in the Highlands of Scotland.

There, as my storytelling mother had done for me, I told tales to my own children. I wrote much also, as poet, journalist, and playwright. But the children wanted "a proper book" out of my stories; and so it was that I began on the fantasy and historical adventure novels that led at last, in 1975, to *The Stronghold* receiving Britain's premier award for children's writers, The Carnegie Medal.

Still in my mind, however, was a young adult novel that seemed absolutely to demand being written—one that I called *A Sound of Chariots* and made largely autobiographical. It being so, also seemed to release in me a new voice that I found I could use for other novels for young adults. And so I followed on with more of these; and in all of them, instead of exploiting research, I drew further on the circumstances of my own life as in *The Third Eye,*

Cat, Herself, and, of course, *Hold on to Love,* the sequel to *A Sound of Chariots.*

It has been more than thrilling for me, also, to have found these young adult novels recognised by critics as well as enjoyed by readers—especially when that first one, *A Sound of Chariots,* resulted in my being paid the honour of being "hung" in The National Portrait Gallery of Scotland in the portrait series "Eminent Scots of the Twentieth Century." In the United States, too, both readers and critics seem to have had the same reaction, and I was further honoured there when the same book meant my becoming the 1992 recipient of the Phoenix Award.

But what of new writers coming up to replace oldsters like me? I pass on to them the best advice I ever had, which was, "Write what you like, how you like. And sooner or later, *if it's good enough,* someone will publish it."

Bibliography

Books for Young Adults

1967	*The Spanish Letters*
1968	*A Pistol in Greenyards*
1969	*Ghosts of Glencoe*
1970	*The Lothian Run*
1971	*The Thirteenth Member*
1972	*A Sound of Chariots*
1974	*The Stronghold*
1979	*The Third Eye*
1981	*You Never Knew Her As I Did*
1983	*Hold on to Love* (in the U.K. as *The Dragonfly Years*)
1985	*Cat, Herself* (in the U.K. as *I'll Go My Own Way*)

Books for Middle Graders

1963	*Smartest Man in Ireland*
1966	*The Kelpies Pearls*
1967	*Thomas and the Warlocks*
1968	*The Ferlie*
1970	*The Walking Stones*
1972	*The Haunted Mountain*
1975	*A Stranger Came Ashore*
1977	*The Wicked One*
1988	*The Mermaid Summer*

Books for Children

1977   *A Furl of Fairy Wind*
1983   *The Knight of the Golden Plain*
1985   *The Three Day Enchantment*

Nonfiction

1976   *Talent Is Not Enough*

Adrienne Jones

PHOTO: GWEN RINEHART

What would you really like to know about a writer?

Since our connection is books, let's start there.

My earliest books were for middle graders. Now I write for young adults. I quarrel with that phrase. I hope you won't refer to me as an old adult! The stories I write are full-fledged novels enjoyed by both YAs and OAs.

You'll find that most "serious" novelists write from their own experiences, emotions, views of life. Thus, in literature, we find a great and wonderful variety. I urge young authors—write about whatever burns in your mind. Live life fully and work at understanding others. Put yourself in another's shoes and it's amazing how life broadens and blooms. *Watch. Listen. Remember.* It will all come alive on your pages. Oh, if only I could chat face to face with each of you about writing. There is so much to say! But, never fear, you'll find your way, for writers are a determined breed.

Yes, I have, indeed, "written from myself." My hometown is Atlanta, Georgia. In *Whistle Down a Dark Lane* and *A Matter of Spunk*, you'll read of my first seven years there; of the breakup of our family; of Mother, Doris (my sister), and me coming to California on the train. We settled in the Hollywood hills at the Theosophical Colony, Krotona. It's all told from seven-year-old Magpie's viewpoint. Magpie: a fictionalized me. But what she sees is far from childish and definitely sets these as books for adults, YA *and* OA. To regard the world through the unblinking gaze of a child is a time-honored way to tell a story. You'll remember that Harper Lee's *To Kill a Mockingbird* lets us see the life of a town and its people through six-year-old Scout's eyes.

Readers tell me that they laugh and cry and shiver over *Whistle* and *Spunk.* What a lovely thing for a writer to hear!

103

Street Family, a contemporary novel of mine, is from another personal concern: the homeless. Research for this was done on Los Angeles's Skid Row, in bus stations, at the county hospital, talking with street people and with those who try to help.

Even my first published book, *Thunderbird Pass*, came from intense personal interests. The setting: California's High Sierra. My fascination with wild places started in Georgia's Blue Ridge Mountains where we summered when I was a child at our vacation home, Cloudacres. So, my heart was "environmental" before "environmentalist" became a popular word.

Mountains brought me another love—my husband, Dick Jones, a fine mountaineer and skier. We met in the Sierra Club. Together, we made the ascent and descent of Mt. Whitney's sheer east face. Later I found that I was the first woman to make that difficult round trip. You will find bits of that climb in *The Hawks of Chelney* and *Long Time Passing*.

We are still happy together after fifty-two years. We have a son, Gregory, a daughter, Gwen, and four grandchildren, Jason, Jaimi, Andy, and Teddy. They enrich our lives.

To all of you: Find adventures in reading! To you writers: Cheers and good fortune! Maybe someday, in a school or library, we'll meet for that face to face chat.

Bibliography

Books for Young Adults

1971   *Another Place, Another Spring*
1974   *The Mural Master*
1974   *So, Nothing Is Forever*
1978   *The Hawks of Chelney*
1980   *The Beckoner*
1982   *Whistle Down A Dark Lane*
1983   *A Matter of Spunk*
1987   *Street Family*
1990   *Long Time Passing*
1992   *Joys of a Dark Decade*

Books for Middle Graders

1952   *Thunderbird Pass*
1957   *Where Eagles Fly*
1964   *Ride the Far Wind*
1966   *Wild Voyageur: Story of a Canada Goose*
1968   *Sail, Calypso!*

Diana Wynne Jones

PHOTO: COLIN BURROW

My childhood was highly unpleasant, although, I see now, exactly adapted to force me to become a writer. When World War II broke out, I was first sent to Wales, which was (and still is) a foreign country, and then to a large house in the English Lakes. This house belonged to John Ruskin's secretary and was the home of the family who figure in Arthur Ransome's books for children. Arthur Ransome himself lived in a houseboat just along the lake, and he objected to the disturbance we children made. He came to complain. He did not like children. Around the same time, Beatrix Potter, who also lived nearby, smacked my sister (aged three) for swinging on her gate. She did not like children, either. Nor, it appeared, did the late John Ruskin. I found a stack of his flower-drawings in the attic and erased them in order to draw on the paper. I was punished for this. Consequently, I grew up with the notion that writers were very real, very powerful, and did not care for children. Even at this time—I was six—I felt that children had a raw deal.

We then moved to a village called Thaxted, in Essex, where my parents ran a Conference Centre. Again, there was no time for children. We never had any books to read. My father, who, in a contest with Scrooge, would have won hands-down, considered he had supplied us with reading when he purchased all the books by Arthur Ransome (him again!), which he locked in a high cupboard and dispensed, one between the three of us, each Christmas. We bicycled miles to find books. In the end, I took to writing stories in old school notebooks and reading them aloud to my sisters. This proved to me I could finish a long work (something every writer needs to be sure of). Oddly enough, these early books said nothing about the village—which contained at least two genuine witches—because this was real life and I preferred fantasy.

When I was older, my father decided that I should learn Greek and be tutored for entry into university. He therefore took away from my two sisters the dolls house a friend had given them and swapped it for lessons for me from a philosophy professor who lived nearby. I had three lessons. Then the philosopher ran away with someone else's wife. But I nevertheless gained a place at Oxford University, where the room I was given had been the studio of John Ruskin (him again!). It was the coldest room in town.

At Oxford, I attended lectures by both J. R. R. Tolkien and C. S. Lewis and was inspired (very differently) by both. Though I retained my penchant for fantasy and my intention of becoming a writer, I imagined at this stage that I would be writing for adults. It was not until I married and had children of my own that I changed my mind.

My children taught me a great deal. With them, I read all the books for children I had not been able to read as a child. All my children had very firm views. Though they loved most classics for children, they had nothing but contempt for most recent books. They wanted books that made them laugh. It was not long before I was trying my hand at writing children's books.

I wrote a great many and sent them to publishers, who sent them back at once with peculiar comments, such as, "You do not say the ages of the children in this book." This had been deliberate on my part. My kids were humiliated if they identified with a character who turned out to be younger than they were. I was doing a lot of deliberate things publishers did not like, because of careful observation of my own children. Another such thing was that I put adult characters in my books who were less than perfect. This, in those days (the *early* '60s) was Against the Rule. The books came back. But eventually, when I was introduced to my agent, things changed. I have now written over twenty-five books and hope to write many more.

Bibliography

Books for Young Adults
1975   *Eight Days of Luke*
1975   *Cart and Cwidder*

1975	*Dogsbody*
1976	*Power of Three*
1977	*Drowned Ammet*
1977	*Charmed Life*
1980	*The Magicians of Caprona*
1981	*The Time of the Ghost*
1984	*Archer's Goon*
1987	*A Tale of Time City*
1989	*Hidden Turnings* (short stories)
1991	*Aunt Maria* (in the U.K., *Black Maria*)

Books for Middle Graders

1973	*Wilkins' Tooth*
1974	*The Ogre Downstairs*
1981	*The Homeward Bounders*
1982	*Witch Week*
1984	*Warlock at the Wheel*
1989	*Chair Person*
1989	*Wild Robert*

Books for Younger Readers

| 1978 | *Who Got Rid of Angus Flint?* |
| 1980 | *The Four Grannies* |

Books for All Ages

1979	*The Spellcoats*
1984	*The Skivers' Guide*
1985	*Fire and Hemlock*
1986	*Howl's Moving Castle*
1988	*The Lives of Christopher Chant*
1990	*Castle in the Air*

Annette Curtis Klause

PHOTO: MORRIS POMERANTZ

I was born in Bristol, in the southwest of England, in 1953. My early literary influences were the classics ("Baa, Baa, Black Sheep," etc.). When I was seven, my family moved up north to Newcastle upon Tyne. It was there I wrote my classic juvenile work, *The Blood Ridden Pool of Solen Goom*. Both the public library and the old science fiction magazines and paperbacks in the spare room held treasure that made me a lifelong avid reader. Reading led naturally to writing, which I did through most of my childhood—poems, plays, and stories.

When I was fifteen, my father's career as a radiologist brought us to Washington, D.C. We were only going to be in this country for a year but we ended up staying. I wrote poetry all through high school and college (at first, soppy love stuff and later, wickedly shocking and tongue-in-cheek) but it wasn't until after I graduated with my master's degree in library science that I started writing fiction again.

I continued writing poetry, often with science fiction and fantasy themes, and had some published in small magazines, but I didn't have much luck with my short stories or picture book manuscripts, so it feels very satisfying that my horror story "The Hoppins" has finally been published (in *Short Circuits*, edited by D. Gallo).

When I decided to write a novel for young adults, I remembered how infatuated I was after reading my first vampire book when I was fourteen. I dug out the embarrassing poem saga about vampires I wrote back then, and when I'd stopped laughing and cringing, I discovered the seeds of my first published novel, *The Silver Kiss*. I even reused one of the poems. Apparently what worked for a teenage girl then works for teenage girls now, because the book has been very successful.

It was natural that I should attempt a science fiction book next, but writing science fiction is much harder than reading it. *The Silver Kiss* was such a visceral story that it just seemed to roll out of me; *Alien Secrets*, however, entailed extensive outlining in order to create a future world that was believable, give the characters background, and make the mystery element in the plot work logically. And then most of the details don't even show up in the book!

My first novel began with an infatuation; my second began with an image of an alien crouched in fear in a corridor as ghosts streamed past (who is this and what is happening? I asked myself); my third book has begun with possession. I'll be driving to work, a heart-thumping rock song will come on the radio, and suddenly I tense, my eyes narrow, my nails and teeth grow longer—a dangerous girl takes me over. She wants me to tell her story, a story of the darker side of teenage sexuality. I'm really enjoying it.

I still work as a children's librarian in Maryland, and live with my husband and four cats—but every so often I turn into a werewolf.

Bibliography

Books for Young Adults
1990   *The Silver Kiss*
1993   *Alien Secrets*

Ron Koertge

I was born in 1940. I spent most of my childhood in Collinsville, Illinois, which is only a few miles from St. Louis, Missouri, but nowhere near as sophisticated or uptown.

It's easy to look back and say that I was likely to become a writer, but that suggests a kind of foresight and inevitability that I'm not sure is appropriate. I chose English as a major in college because I had to choose something. I went to graduate school in Tucson, Arizona, because the University of Arizona was the only school that offered me a teaching assistantship. I started to write poetry there because some of the other teaching assistants wrote poems and submitted them to little magazines. Because I wanted to have something in common with them, I tried writing poems, too. So my career sometimes strikes me as a series of coincidences. This is not a method I'd suggest to any young person, but it worked for me, and it does have a kind of goofy optimism about it; all along I thought things would turn out fine.

My first two Young Adult books came from manuscripts that failed as novels for grown-ups. The next three I wrote because I had, like an ostrich with a single egg, one idea per year. I sometimes wonder what I'll do when and if my annual idea loses its way. Will that mean it's time for me to write something else? Or perhaps nothing at all?

When I was married to my first wife, I fell into the habit of thinking I was in charge of my life. Now I'm less sure. It's fun to write what emerges and to do what comes next. I was discouraged with writing poetry when, in 1990, I won a National Endowment for the Arts fellowship. Clearly, I was not supposed to stop writing poems.

My novels tend to be funny because I was blessed and saddled with a peculiar sense of humor. But because of the frank sexuality of my first three books and because of the gay uncle in *The Arizona Kid*, I'm sometimes called an activist. I don't mind, but the fact is that writing about teenagers makes writing about sex seem inevitable to me, not iconoclastic; Wes turned out to be a gay character because I was walking with my wife (the new one) and I said, "I wonder if it'd be interesting to make the uncle gay?" And I meant interesting for *me*. One of the reasons I write books is to amuse myself, to see what characters will say and how they'll behave. If I know too much about a book in advance, it's less fun, like reading too much about the Grand Canyon and watching videos about it makes finally seeing it pretty blah.

When students ask me about their own writing or their own urges to write, they often talk about how difficult it is to write well; they worry about quality and then they freeze. The way around that—sometimes called writer's block to differentiate it, I guess, from butcher's block—is to write every day and to give up judging. Just write the novel or story or essay or poem and keep writing. Then the block turns out to be sugar, the words turn out to be rain, and everybody knows what happens next.

Bibliography

Books for Young Adults

1986   *Where the Kissing Never Stops*
1988   *The Arizona Kid*
1990   *The Boy in the Moon*
1991   *Mariposa Blues*
1992   *The Harmony Arms*

Books for Adults

1980   *The Boogeyman*

Recent Books of Poetry

1980   *Life on the Edge of the Continent*
1991   *High School Dirty Poems*

E. L. Konigsburg

Although I was born in New York City, my family moved to Pennsylvania when I was only nine months old. I did my growing up in two small towns there: Phoenixville in the east and Farrell in the west. I graduated from Carnegie Mellon University as a chemistry major and attended graduate school at the University of Pittsburgh.

Here are the three major writing lessons I have had:

Beyond high school, the only writing course I had was freshman composition. We were science students, so we were taught to express complicated scientific material in clear, concise language— excellent training for writing fiction as well as fact. I dedicated one of my books to Dr. A. Fred Sochatoff, the professor who taught that course.

Lesson One: *Write in a straightforward manner.*

When we moved to Jacksonville, Florida, I decided to teach. I was not certified to teach in a public school, so I took a position teaching general science and biology at Bartram, a private girls' school. There I learned my next two lessons in writing.

Miss Pratt, who was headmistress of the school, asked me to prepare my first lesson and bring it to her. I wrote an outline of a lecture that included a history of science and a lengthy explanation of the scientific method. Miss Pratt looked over my outline, closed my folder, and said, "I think you should start with water. Yes, water is a good place to start. Show how it cannot be compressed and explain how it keeps us clean and why we have to drink it. Yes," she repeated, "water is a good place to start."

Miss Pratt was right. Water is a good place to start. You cannot explain about water not being compressed without explaining hydraulic pressure; that, of course, leads to an explanation of pressure

113

itself which is best taught by classroom experimentation. Experimentation teaches observation. Observation and experimentation are the cornerstones of the scientific method. While learning how discoveries are made, students also learn some history of science.

Lesson Two: Start with water. *Go from the specific to the general, not vice versa.*

As I was growing up, I knew of only two kinds of private schools, parochial and military. It was not until I entered college that I learned that there were private schools where rich people traditionally sent their kids to prepare them for college. I had not met many graduates of these prep schools at Carnegie Mellon; I knew none of them well, and my opinion of them could be summed up as follows: they had more cashmere sweaters than the rest of us.

Now I was scheduled to teach them. I expected to find a lot of spoiled brats. I was wrong. What I found was that once the matter of food and clothing—once the problem of basic needs is answered—these rich girls in private schools were asking themselves the same questions I had asked myself as I was growing up poor in public schools in Pennsylvania: Who am I? What makes me the same as everyone else? What makes me different from everyone else? These are the questions I still ask.

Lesson Three: Write clearly, write concisely, write about specific incidents and specific characters, but *ask big questions.*

Notice, please, I have said nothing about talent and nothing about the discipline it takes to apply that talent. I assume that if you've read this far, you have as much of those as you need.

Bibliography

Books for Children and Young Adults

1967   *Jennifer, Hecate, Macbeth, William McKinley, and Me, Elizabeth*
1967   *From the Mixed-Up Files of Mrs. Basil E. Frankweiler*
1969   *About the B'nai Bagels*
1970   *(George)*
1971   *Altogether, One at a Time* (short stories)
1973   *A Proud Taste for Scarlet and Miniver*
1974   *The Dragon in the Ghetto Caper*
1975   *The Second Mrs. Giaconda*
1976   *Father's Arcane Daughter*
1979   *Throwing Shadows* (short stories)
1982   *Journey to an 800 Number*

114

Louise Lawrence

Being asked to write an autobiography left me instantly stymied . . . because as an entity Louise Lawrence does not exist . . . and who wants to know about me? I just live the life . . . she creates the books. But my hand is her hand, so there must be a point where we meet, where I'm her and she's me.

She certainly wasn't there when I was born on June 5, 1943, in Leatherhead in Surrey. I was named Elizabeth, played games with my own shadow, was asthmatic and solitary, steeped in fairy tales, and afraid of everyone. Primary school was a bad experience, and I was glad to leave it behind.

We moved to the Forest of Dean in Gloucestershire when I was twelve years old. No one knew me so I assumed a different personality. I became Liz who was not afraid of anyone. People accepted me, and the five years I spent at Lydney Grammar School were a good experience.

I quit, aged seventeen, and worked in a library, fell in love with books and the wrong man, married, lived in an isolated farmhouse and bred children . . . three in three years. Motherhood was hard work and marriage was another bad experience. I painted pictures to keep myself intact and had no ambitions to be a writer.

Washing diapers . . . that's when it happened . . . suddenly, unexpectedly, out of the blue. It was as if I had a movie screen inside my head and I watched the movie unfold, a set of characters acting out their story. It was all quite distinct . . . everything they said, everything they did, the landscape through which they moved, names, faces, places. "That would make a good book," I thought. So I wrote it down, typed it out, put the name of the author on the binder . . . *Louise Lawrence*, born in 1966 between the second and third child.

It was not a very good book after all . . . but the next one was better, and the next one better still. She had to learn how to write by trial and error, and I had to learn how not to exist so that the characters we wrote about could live instead of me. It was a wonderful way to escape from a reality which was becoming unbearable. For days, weeks, months on end I could cease to be myself . . . let Louise Lawrence take over, travel time and the universe, create books from the visions that entered my head.

In 1970 *Andra* was accepted for publication and Louise Lawrence became a professional writer. I left my marriage behind, raised kids, dug gardens, worked in a restaurant, went fruit-picking in the fields, and she went on writing . . . *Cat Call, Star Lord, The Earth Witch* . . . together we survived.

I grew to depend on her. Her writing improved and I gave her more and more of my time. The movies in my head kept happening and book followed book . . . *Children of the Dust, Moonwind, The Warriors of Taan*. I thought it would go on forever, but I suppose it was inevitable that my own life should intrude.

My own life . . . that was never Louise Lawrence's province. Mine were the little scraps of years where the children grew to adulthood and left to live their own lives. Mine was the remaining loneliness where no one was. I gave up writing to look after my mother who was sick, then left to marry a man with whom I could be happy.

Good years living my own life, enjoying companionship, working together to renovate a derelict house, realising the value of human friendship, a physical existence . . . Louise Lawrence, writer, could have no place in that. And why should I want to give it all up for her? Why should I want to write books when I was happily engaged in real living? We reached an impasse, she and I, not wanting to know each other.

It has not come easy, learning to be a writer again. I returned to it reluctantly, knowing I was qualified to earn a living in no other way. I can give it some of my time, but never again will I give it all of my time. Human contact is too sweet to relinquish for the written word. I have to make room for both. Books happen more slowly and much less surely, but I am beginning to enjoy writing once again.

Now I write for a different purpose . . . not to escape from reality, not driven to express the visions in my head, and not for financial survival (although that does provide a certain incentive). I write because I choose to, of my own free will. I am not as dedicated as Louise Lawrence, but then, I'm not her and never was. But she's me for a few hours a day until we've finished the next novel.

Bibliography

Books for Young Adults
1970   *Andra*
1972   *The Power of Stars*

Ursula K. Le Guin

PHOTO: © MARIAN KOLISCH 1988

I was born in 1920 in Berkeley, California, where I grew up. My parents were the anthropologist Alfred Kroeber and the author Theodora Kroeber, author of *Ishi*. I went to Radcliffe College and did graduate work at Columbia University, then married Charles A. Le Guin, a historian, in Paris in 1953. We have lived in Portland, Oregon, since 1958, and have three children and a grandchild.

I have written poetry and fiction all my life. My first publications were poems, and in the 1960s I began to publish short stories and novels. I write both poetry and prose, and in several modes or "genres," including realistic fiction, science fiction, fantasy, young children's books, books for young adults, screenplays, essays, verbal texts for musicians, and voicetexts for performance or recording. As of 1992, I have published over eighty short stories (many collected in four volumes), two collections of essays, three volumes of poetry, and sixteen novels. Among the honors my writing has received are a National Book Award, five Hugos, four Nebulas, the Kafka Award, and a Pushcart Prize.

My occupations are writing, reading, housework, and teaching. I am a feminist, a conservationist, and a Western American, passionately involved with West Coast literature, landscape, and life.

When I began writing for young adults, my first book was a fantasy about a young wizard (*A Wizard of Earthsea*). Back then, wizards were always old geezers with white beards, and I began wondering what they were like as teenagers. This led me into the whole world of Earthsea, and three more books eventually followed.

My novel *Very Far Away from Anywhere Else* is not a fantasy, but a story about ordinary, bright high school kids in the 1970s.

Two of my books were not published as young adult but are

often discovered by young adult readers: *The Eye of the Heron,* which is science fiction, and *The Beginning Place,* which combines gritty realism and "escapist" fantasy in a fairly explosive mixture.

I get a good many letters from young women and men who want to be writers, asking for advice and help. It would be really nice to have some magic words for the would-be writers, but I know only two that will really work the spell:

1. Write.
2. Read.

Believe me, it works.

Bibliography

Books for Young Adults

1968	*A Wizard of Earthsea*
1970	*The Tombs of Atuan*
1972	*The Farthest Shore*
1976	*Very Far Away from Anywhere Else*
1980	*The Beginning Place*
1983	*The Eye of the Heron*
1990	*Tehanu: The Last Book of Earthsea*

Books for Children

1979	*Leese Webster,* illus. by James Brunsman
1983	*Cobbler's Rune*
1988	*Solomon Leviathan,* illus. by A. Austin
1988	*A Visit from Dr. Katz,* illus. by A. Barrow
1988	*Catwings,* illus. by J. Schindler
1989	*Catwings Returns,* illus. by J. Schindler
1989	*Fire and Stone,* illus. by Laura Marshall

Short Story Collections

1975	*The Wind's Twelve Quarters*
1976	*Orsinian Tales*
1982	*The Compass Rose*
1987	*Buffalo Gals*
1991	*Searoad*

Poetry Collections

| 1974 | *Wild Angels* |
| 1981 | *Hard Words* |

| 1983 | "In the Red Zone" (with artist Henk Pander) |
| 1988 | *Wild Oats and Fireweed* |

Anthologies Edited

1977	*Nebula Award Stories XI*
1980	*Interfaces* (with Virginia Kidd)
1980	*Edges* (with Virginia Kidd)

Books for Adults

1966	*Rocannon's World*
1966	*Planet of Exile*
1967	*City of Illusion*
1969	*The Left Hand of Darkness*
1971	*The Lathe of Heaven*
1974	*The Dispossessed*
1976	*The Word for World is Forest*
1979	*Malafrena*
1982	*The Language of the Night* (criticism)
1985	*Always Coming Home,* illus. by Margaret Chodos; music by Todd Barton
1985	*King Dog* (screenplay)
1989	*Dancing at the Edge of the World* (criticism)

Sonia Levitin

PHOTO: ROSE EICHENBAUM

I teach creative writing in adult education, and have done so for many years. Students often ask me, "Is this a good time to be a writer?" And I always respond with a resounding, "Never better!"

Inwardly, I laugh at the question. How can any time be better or worse than the one in which we are living? And what difference does it make what the "experts" say? We live when we are born; we do the thing we are cut out to do. I was meant to be a writer, I feel sure of that. In metaphor, I think of myself as a bridge—a bridge between generations and between cultures, between all kinds of people. In my books I try to reach over to clasp their hands and especially to touch their hearts.

I was born into a dangerous place in a dangerous time. I am a child of the Holocaust. I am sickened and furious at the evil perpetrated in Germany, the place of my birth. But do I regret my birth? Of course not. We all live our lives as they are given. We must accept our personal past and use it in the best way we can. Every life has its injustice and its glory.

When I was four years old, I was brought to America. This in itself was something of a miracle, and I am thankful for it daily. I grew up in Los Angeles, strangely caught between two worlds, the old and the new, Europe and America, parents and new friends. These experiences are the theme and the inspiration for many of my novels: the pull of adventure, the hope of improvement, the lure of change, contrasted by the tug of the old ways, the expectations of family and clan. One learns to balance. That is the secret of living well.

I have worked as a camp counselor, a teacher, a writer. I always knew I would work with and for children in some way. At the age of twelve, I decided to become a writer. One of the most rewarding aspects of being a writer is the freedom to think and study, to read the works of great thinkers and doers, to imagine and create different small worlds. Being absorbed in writing a book, in its characters and ideas, is a delicious feeling of being truly alive, involved not in the self, but in the living force we call creativity. It feels great, like skiing down a mountain or running five miles.

I have a good home, a wonderful husband, two fine children, and the ability to do work that I love. Of course, I've had troubles along the way. Trouble and conflict are the raw materials of fiction. To translate life's problems into dramatic fiction is a superb therapy, as well as my chosen art.

I love to write. I hate rejection. What else is new? No artist can ever be said to have "arrived." There are always greater and more difficult challenges just ahead. I hope to write until the very last day of my life. Since my mother is still healthy at the age of ninety-four, perhaps I have many, many more books in store.

As I continue after thirty years of writing (twenty-one years of publishing books), I realize that I am getting deeper into my heritage, my Jewishness, looking to my roots for both emotional and intellectual nourishment.

I like to take long hikes in the country or by the shore, especially with our two dogs. Our favorite times are spent with our grown children, Daniel and Shari, and with good friends. I also enjoy skiing, jogging, reading, studying, and traveling. I have seen nearly all of Europe, some of Asia, and I have taken four marvelous trips to Israel. I love to entertain everybody at holiday time, and we always have the Passover Seder here, as well as other festive Jewish holidays.

If anybody asks me what it takes to be a writer, I reply, first, a love of words and drama. Second, a constant and growing awareness of the world and the people in it. Third, fourth, and fifth, perseverance, perseverance, perseverance.

Bibliography

Books for Young Adults

1970	*Journey to America*
1973	*Roanoke, A Novel of the Lost Colony*
1976	*The Mark of Conte*
1977	*Beyond Another Door*

1978	*The No-Return Trail*
1982	*The Year of Sweet Senior Insanity*
1984	*Smile Like a Plastic Daisy*
1986	*A Season for Unicorns*
1987	*The Return*
1988	*Incident at Loring Groves*
1989	*Silver Days*
1992	*The Golem and the Dragon Girl*
1993	*Annie's Year*

Books for Middle Graders

1971	*Rita the Weekend Rat*
1974	*Jason and the Money Tree*

Picture Books

1973	*Who Owns the Moon?*
1976	*A Single Speckled Egg*
1979	*A Sound to Remember*
1980	*Nobody Stole the Pie*
1982	*The Fisherman and the Bird*
1982	*All the Cats in the World*
1991	*The Man Who Kept His Heart in a Bucket*
1993	*A Piece of Home*

Books for Adults

1976	*Reigning Cats and Dogs*
1981	*What They Did to Miss Lily* (as Sonia Wolff)

Lois Lowry

I've always felt that I was fortunate to have been born the middle child of three. My older sister, Helen, was very much like our mother: gentle, family-oriented, eager to please. Little brother Jon was the only boy and had interests that he shared with our father; together they were always working on electric trains and erector sets, and later, they always seemed to have their heads under the raised hood of a car.

That left me in-between, and exactly where I wanted to be: on my own. I was a solitary child who lived in the world of books and my own imagination.

Because my father was a career military officer—an army dentist—I lived all over the world. I was born in Hawaii, moved from there to New York, spent the years of World War II in my mother's Pennsylvania hometown, and from there went to Tokyo when I was eleven. High school was back in New York City, but by the time I went to college (Brown University in Rhode Island), my family was living in Washington, D.C.

I married young. Women did that so often in those days. I had just had my nineteenth birthday—and finished my sophomore year in college—when I married a naval officer and continued the odyssey that military life requires. California. Connecticut. Florida. South Carolina. Finally Cambridge, Massachusetts, when my husband left the service and entered Harvard Law School; and then to Maine— by this time with four children under age five in tow.

My children grew up in Maine. So did I. I returned to college at the University of Southern Maine, got my degree, went to graduate school, and finally began to write professionally, the thing I had dreamed of doing since those childhood years when I had endlessly scribbled stories and poems into notebooks.

After my marriage ended in 1977, when I was forty, I settled into the life I have led ever since. I spend my days happily alone, reading and writing. I live and work in Boston, in the old section of the city called Beacon Hill, where the sidewalks are bumpy and brick and the streetlights are still gas, as they were a century ago. Weekends, I go to New Hampshire, where I have an old brick farmhouse surrounded by flower gardens, woods, and birds.

My books have varied in content and style. Yet it seems to me that all of them deal, essentially, with the same general theme: the importance of human connections. *A Summer to Die*, my first book, is a fictionalized retelling of the early death of my sister, and of the effect of such a loss on a family. *Number the Stars*, set in a different culture and era, tells of the same things: the role that we humans play in the lives of our fellow beings.

A new book, not yet published, tentatively titled *The Giver*, takes place against the background of yet another very different culture and time. Though broader in scope than my earlier books, it nonetheless speaks to the same concern: the vital need for humans to be aware of their interdependence, not only with each other but with the world and its environment.

I think it is my own children, all of them grown now, who have caused me to expand my view. One of my sons is a fighter pilot in the United States Air Force; as a mother during the recent Gulf War, I was newly stunned into a fear for the world and a heightened awareness of the necessity to find a way to end conflict. One of my daughters has become disabled as the result of a disease of the central nervous system; through her, I have a new and passionate awareness of the importance of human connections that transcend physical differences.

And I have a grandson now. For him, and for my grandchildren not yet born, I feel a greater urgency to do what I can to convey the knowledge that we live intertwined on this planet and that our future as human beings depends upon our caring more, and doing more, for one another.

Bibliography

Books for Young Adults
1977   *A Summer to Die*
1978   *Find a Stranger, Say Goodbye*
1980   *Autumn Street*

1983	*Taking Care of Terrific*
1992	*The Giver*

Books for Middle Graders

1978	*Anastasia Krupnik*
1981	*Anastasia Again!*
1982	*Anastasia at Your Service*
1983	*The 100th Thing About Caroline*
1984	*Anastasia, Ask Your Analyst*
1984	*Us and Uncle Fraud*
1985	*Switcharound*
1986	*Anastasia Has the Answers*
1987	*Anastasia on Her Own*
1987	*Rabble Starkey*
1988	*Anastasia's Chosen Career*
1989	*All About Sam*
1990	*Number the Stars*
1991	*Your Move, J. P.!*
1991	*Anastasia At This Address*
1992	*Attaboy, Sam!*

Stephen Manes

I'm a child of the television generation, born in Pittsburgh in 1949, when TV was black-and-white and new and not everybody had one. When I was three and my parents bought their first TV set, it became a major factor in my life. For one thing, it helped teach me to read, mainly by watching the commercials. I can still sing the jingles for Duquesne Beer ("Have a Duke!") and Wilkens Jewelers ("E-Z Credit! E-Z Credit! Wilkens is the place where you can get it!"), which shows what TV did to my brain.

Because I knew how to read, the second-grade teacher at my four-room school sat me down in front of her typewriter, handed me an exercise book, and had me learn to type, something I never mastered until computers came along years later. But when my family moved, my two-finger hunt-and-pecking got me the job of roving reporter with my new school's newspaper. My specialty was humor, and I won statewide second prizes for it. I even started a novel—*Ping-Pong Champs*—but never managed to finish it. I had hoped to become an astronaut, but in sixth grade I became editor-in-chief of the *Sunnyside Review*.

In high school, torn between publishing, photography, and ping-pong, I led a futile attempt to launch a literary magazine—a project that our pea-brained faculty advisor censored and ultimately killed. I had better luck at the University of Chicago, where I ran the film society and founded *Focus!*, a maverick journal on film criticism and snottiness.

I studied cinema at the University of Southern California, and then wrote a variety of documentary TV shows and unproduced movies. When one of my scripts was rewritten, retitled, and released as an awful mess called *Mother, Jugs, and Speed,* I decided maybe it was time for a career change.

128

My first wife, a children's librarian, had been bringing home exciting books for kids, so I decided to try my hand at writing them. In the beginning, my manuscripts were rejected so often I could tell them from the way they sounded when the mailman poked them through the mail slot. But my first book, *Mule in the Mail*, eventually led to more than thirty—so far.

Writing has been my professional life more than twenty years. In some ways, it can be the best job in the world: an easy commute, flexible hours, tremendous variety. But there are drawbacks: Nobody pays you for vacation or sick leave—or for just showing up. And you have to be able to cope with rejection. Some of my most popular books have received horrible reviews. One of my favorite manuscripts was finally published ten years after I originally wrote it, after being rejected more than twenty-five times.

What I like best about writing books is that they're personal. Filmmakers can change anything a writer puts down on paper. A book is your own invention: the words are all yours. And knowing you've created something out of thin air that people enjoy and understand and maybe even laugh at is a thrill that artists and inventors and craftspeople cherish, but very few others are lucky enough to experience. I love being able to point to my books and say proudly, "They're mine. I did them. They're pretty good." And I do!

Bibliography

Books for Young Adults
1981	*Slim Down Camp*
1982	*I'll Live*
1982	*Unbirthday* (as A. M. Stephensen)
1983	*Video War*
1988	*The Obnoxious Jerks*
1992	*Comedy High*

Books for Middle Graders
1978	*Hooples on the Highway*
1979	*The Boy who Turned into a TV Set*
1981	*The Hooples' Haunted House*
1982	*Be a Perfect Person In Just Three Days!*
1982	*Pictures of Motion and Pictures That Move: Eadweard Muybridge and the Photography of Motion*

1982   *Socko! Every Riddle Your Feet Will Ever Need*
1983   *That Game from Outer Space*
1984   *The Oscar J. Noodleman Television Network*
1984   *Computer Monsters* (with Paul Somerson)
1984   *Computer Olympics* (with Paul Somerson)
1984   *Computer Space Adventures* (with Paul Somerson)
1984   *Computer Craziness* (with Paul Somerson)
1985   *Life is No Fair!*
1986   *The Hooples' Horrible Holiday*
1987   *Chicken Trek*
1988   *The Great Gerbil Roundup*
1989   *Monstra vs. Irving*
1989   *It's New! It's Improved! It's Terrible!*
1990   *Chocolate-Covered Ants*
1990   *Some of the Adventures of Rhode Island Red*
1991   *Make Four Million Dollars By Next Thursday!*

Books for Younger Readers

1978   *Mule in the Mail*
1983   *The Bananas Move to the Ceiling* (With Esther Manes)

Books for Adults

1985   *Encyclopedia Placematica* (with Ron Barrett)
1987   *StarFixer* (with Paul Somerson)
1988   *The Complete MCI Mail Handbook*
1992   *Gates: How Microsoft's Mogul Reinvented an Industry and Became the Richest Man in America* (with Paul Andrews)

Ann M. Martin

hile I was growing up in Princeton, New Jersey, I never thought about becoming a published author. Instead, I planned to become an elementary school teacher, and I did teach a fourth/fifth-grade class after graduating from Smith College. Then I began work as an editor of children's books for both Scholastic and Bantam and started work on my own novel. It took me three years to finish *Bummer Summer*, but writing has become easier since then.

During college, I spent my summers working as a therapist with autistic children. They and their families were very special to me, and writing about them in *Inside Out* seemed natural.

Then, in 1985, at the urging of an editor at Scholastic, I began working on what has become the Baby-sitters Club, a series about the friendship of seven young girls who provide a baby-sitting service. I included a few actual incidents that had happened to me or one of my friends during my own baby-sitting days. Several years later, I began the Baby-sitters Little Sister series, following the adventures of Karen, the younger stepsister of Kristy Thomas, founder of the Baby-sitters Club.

Writing two books per month for the Baby-sitters Club and Little Sister series is very demanding on my time, especially when I also try to read and respond to the nearly 15,000 letters I receive from readers each year. But like my father, who was a self-employed cartoonist for the *New Yorker*, I am a very disciplined person, and usually work on two or three books at a time, including individual novels not part of the series. If I get stuck on one, I can always move to the other. For me, the writing process is constantly changing and developing.

Bibliography

Books for Children and Young Adults

1983   *Bummer Summer*
1984   *Inside Out*
1985   *Stage Fright*
1985   *Me and Katie (the Pest)*
1986   *With You and Without You*
1986   *Missing Since Monday*
1987   *Just a Summer Romance*
1987   *Slam Book*
1988   *Ten Kids, No Pets*
1988   *Yours Truly, Shirley*
1989   *Ma and Pa Dracula*
1991   *Eleven Kids, One Summer*
1992   *Rachel Parker, Kindergarten Show-Off*

Series
1986–   Baby-sitters Club
1988–   Baby-sitters Little Sister

Carolyn Meyer

I like to write novels, inventing characters and making up stories. I also like to write non-fiction, digging up facts and tracking down details. Everybody expects me to do a lot of research for my nonfiction books. But sometimes it surprises people that I do just as much homework for my novels. As you might expect, much of that homework takes place in a library. But a lot of it is a matter of luck, of finding the right people and asking the right questions.

When I wrote *Killing the Kudu*, I needed to learn what it means to have a paralyzing spinal injury. My local library had almost nothing about it, but I ended up working with the staff at a rehabilitation hospital, as well as talking with paraplegics. *Wild Rover* meant touring a state penitentiary, hanging around a music camp, reading books about the wilderness where the story was set, hiking, and rock climbing—and talking with an ex-convict who had done time.

Before I started *Elliott & Win*, I visited a Big Brothers organization and a kung fu studio and went camping where my characters did. I also studied up on kayaking, quicksand, wildflowers of New Mexico, plastic surgery, and Mozart opera.

Denny's Tapes plunged me into an exploration of black history and culture. Before Denny arrived at his grandmother's house in Chicago, I had read biographies of Langston Hughes, Paul Robeson, and Marian Anderson, pored over maps to plot Denny's route and side trips across the country, and reread Shakespeare's *Othello*.

In preparation for writing the Hotline series, I enrolled in a month-long intensive training course at the local mental health center. Then I volunteered for the suicide prevention hotline, taking a four-hour shift once a week for a year. And before *Because of Lissa* took shape, I began spending time at a large, multiethnic high school, sitting in on classes and listening to teachers and kids, and finding out how high school newspapers work (not the same as when I was a youthful editor!).

So I do my homework, and I try to get it right. But sometimes, even with all the hours and hours of research, I blow it. When I was working on *Elliott & Win* and knew that I would send man and boy off to an opera, I decided to make it *The Magic Flute*, which I had once seen performed. To refresh my memory, I got a book about *The Magic Flute* from the library, so that my description would be accurate. But I missed something.

The man who served as a model for Elliott called me almost immediately after he had received his copy. "It's very good," he said. "But *The Magic Flute* is sung in *German*. On page nineteen you say it's sung in Italian. You should have known better, Carolyn."

Well, I should have. That's the kind of thing I try to avoid. Mostly, I think, I do.

Bibliography

Books for Young Adults

1979	*C. C. Poindexter*
1982	*Eulalia's Island*
1983	*The Summer I Learned About Life*
1984	*The Luck of Texas McCoy*
1986	*Elliott & Win*
1987	*Denny's Tapes*
1989	*Wild Rover*
1990	*Killing the Kudu*
1990	*Because of Lissa*
1990	*The Problem with Sidney*
1991	*Gillian's Choice*
1991	*The Two Faces of Adam*

Books for Middle Graders

1990	*Japan: How Do Hands Make Peace?* (Earth Inspector series)
1992	*Where the Broken Heart Still Beats: The Story of Cyntha Ann Parker*
1993	*White Lilacs*
1993	*Rio Grande Stories*

Nonfiction for Young Adults

1975	*People Who Make Things: How American Craftsmen Live and Work*
1976	*Amish People: Plain Living in A Complex World*
1977	*Eskimos: Growing Up in A Changing Culture*
1980	*The Center: From A Troubled Past to A New Life*
1980	*Rock Band: Big Men in a Great Big Town*
1985	*The Mystery of the Ancient Maya* (with Charles Gallenkamp)
1986	*Voices of South Africa: Growing Up in a Troubled Land*
1987	*Voices of Northern Ireland: Growing Up in a Troubled Land*
1988	*A Voice from Japan: An Outsider Looks In*

Nonfiction for Younger Readers

1969	*Miss Patch's Learn-to-Sew Book*
1970	*Stitch by Stitch: Needlework for Beginners*
1971	*The Bread Book*
1972	*Yarn: The Things It Makes and How to Make Them*
1973	*Saw, Hammer, and Paint*
1974	*Christmas Crafts*
1974	*Milk, Butter, and Cheese*
1975	*Rock Tumbling*
1975	*The Needlework Book of Bible Stories*
1976	*Lots and Lots of Candy*
1976	*Coconut, The Tree of Life*
1977	*Being Beautiful*
1978	*Mask Magic*

Betty Miles

BETTY MILES WITH GRANDDAUGHTER KATIE, 4/92

R eaders sometimes ask me if I liked to write when I was their age. I tell them I did. I've always liked to write, for the same reasons that I like to talk: to say what I think and how I feel. In elementary school—Lockwood School, in Webster Groves, Missouri—I liked to write jokes, poems, letters, book reviews, stories for the school paper, notes to my friends. Everything I wrote was short, never more than a page or two. I would have been astonished back then if you'd told me I would write a real book someday. But all that writing was good practice for becoming an author.

So was working on the Webster High newspaper and the student paper at Antioch College and writing, while I was in college, for a small-town weekly newspaper and a sports magazine. I didn't become a journalist; a teaching job made me want to write books for younger readers. But I still try to write clearly, the way a good reporter does, and—even in my fiction—to get the facts straight.

Reading is also good practice for writing. I was the kind of kid who always had her nose in a book, and I'm that kind of adult, too.

I read everything: newspapers, novels, reports, advertisements, comic strips. I get ideas for books from my reading, and I also get tips on writing: how to write a first page or end a chapter or get a character up and dressed and out of the house in the morning. How to show what a character is feeling.

But it's not only writing and reading that help you become an author—just about any experiences you have can be useful. Being an only child, being a mother, climbing a mountain, talking on TV, what I know about, all of these have turned up in my books. I write about things I remember, like learning to ride a bike at the embarrassing age of ten, as Patty does in *I Would If I Could*; and things I care about, like the environment, which is the subject of my nonfiction handbook *Save the Earth*. My books are full of things I've learned from my three kids, like basketball rules (*All It Takes Is Practice*) and baby-sitting problems (*Just the Beginning*) and the behavior of chickens (*Sink or Swim*), and I'm sure my three granddaughters will teach me new things to write about.

My husband and I live in the house our kids grew up in, in Rockland County, New York, a suburb of New York City. We have a cat named Charles, who hasn't yet appeared in a book. I work at home in a small office, wearing old pants and sweaters and rubber flip-flops. One thing I like about writing is not having to wear real shoes. But I also like to put them on and go out to meet my readers—that's another real pleasure of being a writer.

Bibliography

Books for Middle Graders

1974   *The Real Me*
1974   *Save the Earth: An Ecology Handbook for Kids*
1976   *Just the Beginning*
1976   *All It Takes Is Practice*
1978   *Looking On*
1979   *The Trouble with Thirteen*
1980   *Maudie and Me and the Dirty Book*
1981   *The Secret Life of the Underwear Champ*
1982   *I Would If I Could*
1986   *Sink or Swim*
1991   *Save the Earth: An Action Handbook for Kids*

Picture Books

1958   *A House for Everyone*
1958   *What Is the World*
1959   *The Cooking Book*
1959   *Having a Friend*
1960   *A Day of Summer*
1961   *A Day of Winter*
1961   *Mr. Turtle's Mystery*
1963   *The Feast on Sullivan Street*
1967   *A Day of Autumn*
1967   *Joe Finds a Way* (with Joan Blos)
1970   *A Day of Spring*
1971   *Just Think* (with Joan Blos)
1975   *Around and Around–Love*

Louise Moeri

PHOTO: GLENN KAHL

Not long ago, I met a man who was astonished that I write my books "all by myself." He described writers who had back-up teams to read manuscripts, to criticize, and, above all, to offer support. *I* was astonished to hear that anyone needed—or even allowed—others to help him or her write a book. Other than the fine editors who have pounded several lessons into my skull, I've been going it alone for the better part of forty years. I doubt if any team of expert helpers could have influenced my performance much, since I am a furiously solitary thinker and writer. The committee approach might work for some, but I don't know what a committee could do with my notes scribbled on old grocery lists, used envelopes, and paper towels when that's all I can reach. I am a writer who wakes up at 2:00 a.m. and scrawls a single word which, next morning, grows into a scene, somewhat like those crystal gardens grow out of a dab of dead-looking crumbs in a bowl.

I was born in 1924 in Oregon and have been a westerner—read that "hillbilly"—all my life. I started this one-woman writing operation in high school, continued in college, paused in 1946 to marry and then have three children, and returned to writing when the children were all quite young. I worked full-time, ran a home, raised kids, juggled husband and elderly parents, and wrote. Every so often I quit writing. When the tide of rejections and the workload got too hopeless, I vowed to stop. But I always went back and pulled it all out of the wastebasket and started over.

I realize now that I was born to write, and I would have had to write if it meant scratching the words in a mud flat at low tide.

When I visit classrooms to give "writer's talks," the students ask, "How do you get your ideas?" The answer is that I simply

139

can't fight them off. Literally anything—TV commercials, jokes, chance conversations, falling down the stairs, or having my car break down—will set off that *ping!* in my head and before I know it, I've got three or four characters and a plot unwinding. Most never go much beyond the *ping!*, but a lot have, and no doubt a lot more will, as long as I can hold a pencil and then chain myself to my typewriter to translate them into readable form.

My three children are grown now, and I am the enthusiastic grandmother of a clutch of wild little boys. My husband is now quite handicapped, but I've learned to repair fences with coat hangers, fill the radiator on my car, and get Husband up off the ground when he falls. I'm still writing—alone—and if something doesn't stop me I may yet write a Great American Novel. And if I don't do that, I'll go right on turning out books for kids.

I just can't help it.

Bibliography

1957   *Star Mother's Youngest Child,* illus. by Trina Schart Hyman
1977   *How the Rabbit Stole the Moon,* illus. by Marc Brown
1977   *A Horse for X. Y. Z.,* illus. by Gail Owens
1979   *The Girl Who Lived on the Ferris Wheel*
1981   *Save Queen of Sheba*
1982   *First the Egg*
1982   *The Unicorn and the Plow,* illus. by Diane Goode
1984   *Downwind*
1986   *Journey to the Treasure*
1989   *The Forty-Third War*

Shirley Rousseau Murphy

I grew up in California, near the sea. My father trained horses, and I learned to ride when I was five. I was a solitary child, and I loved riding alone over the green hills and through groves of eucalyptus trees and down sandy riverbeds. I rode in parades and in horse shows, but the best thing was to ride my pony bareback in the sea with the waves crashing around us.

On rainy days I visited my grandparents' house and read from their hundreds of books, or I helped my grandmother make homemade noodles or pies, or she sewed for me. That house was a treasure of attics crammed full of old trunks and old strange clothes; it had tall rooms with Chinese rugs and furniture carved with leaves and winged beasts, rooms that suggested imaginary countries. It was there I first dreamed of dragons.

My mother was a painter, so it was natural for me to draw and paint. I often went sketching with her; we would pack a lunch and drive down the coast beside winter hills where cattle grazed. When I grew up I went to art school. Then I got married, my husband started school under the G.I. Bill, and I worked as a commercial artist. We were poor. We would have been richer if I'd had a more practical skill too, like plumbing or secretarial or electrical work, that pays better and is always in demand—it's handy to have other talents to complement the work of the imagination. No job is menial. I cleaned stalls when I was a child, mended fences, soaped saddles. Simple work is satisfying, and it can teach a great many surprising things.

When my husband graduated and began his own career, I quit my job and began to paint and to do welded sculpture. We don't have any children. For the next eight years I exhibited extensively on the West Coast, then when I was thirty-five we moved to Panama, where there were few galleries for my work. I stopped painting and welding, got a job in the library, and set out to see if I could write.

I hadn't taken any writing courses, but I was determined. I read my way through the children's room of the library, did a lot of thinking, and bought a typewriter. As a painter I had worked long hours every day, and now I did the same as a writer, pounding away far into the night and on weekends. My childhood offered fragments of story on which to build. The sea was in my first books, and the feel of the green land, and my mustang pony. Later came the imagined countries and the dragons, but now the dragons spoke for the grown-up me as well as for my child self.

A strange thing happens when you write: you discover what you truly think; you find out what your heart means. In setting words to paper, you touch something within yourself that you might find in no other way. Writing is not a profession so much as a way of seeing and of growing, and maybe of staying young.

Bibliography

Books for Young Adults

1976   *The Grass Tower*
1977   *The Ring of Fire*
1979   *The Wolf Bell*
1980   *The Castle of Hape*
1981   *Caves of Fire and Ice*
1981   *The Joining of the Stone*
1986   *Nightpool*
1987   *The Ivory Lyre*
1988   *The Dragonbards*
1989   *Medallion of the Black Hound* (with Welch Suggs)

Books for Middle Graders

1967   *White Ghost Summer*
1967   *The Sand Ponies*
1970   *Elmo Doolan and the Search for the Golden Mouse*
1971   *Carlos Charles* (with Patrick Murphy)
1974   *Poor Jenny, Bright as a Penny*
1977   *Silver Woven in My Hair*

1978   *The Flight of the Fox*
1979   *Soonie and the Dragon*
1990   *The Song of the Christmas Mouse*

Books for Younger Readers
1978   *The Pig Who Could Conjure the Wind*
1980   *Mrs. Tortino's Return to the Sun* (with Patrick Murphy), illus.
        by Susan Russo
1983   *Tattie's River Journey,* illus. by Tomie de Paola
1984   *Valentine for a Dragon,* illus. by Kay Chorao
1993   *Wind Child,* illus. by Leo and Diane Dillon

Books for Adults
1991   *The Catswold Portal*

Beverley Naidoo

I was born and brought up "a Jo'burg girl," with the usual notions of most white South Africans, completely taking for granted the service of our cook-cum-nanny, whose own three children lived 300 kilometres away, cared for by . . . I don't know. She provided much of my actual mothering. We knew her as "Mary." I didn't know her real Tswana name. What I do recall, quite vividly, was how, when I was perhaps eight or nine, Mary received a telegram and collapsed. Two of her three young daughters had died. It was diphtheria— something for which I, of course, had been vaccinated.

It was only years later that I began to realise the meaning of that scene. My education took place after I left school, not in any classroom. The early 1960s was a time of political ferment and repression. Apartheid laws had stopped all but a few black students from attending the University of the Witwatersrand. However, along with a small number of politically aware white students, they challenged my inability to see what was all around me. How was it I had been so blind? Struggling to learn to see, I became involved in anti-apartheid activity. In 1964, my detention for eight weeks in solitary confinement, under the "90 days" law, was part of my education. After all, for black South Africans, the country itself was a vast jail.

At twenty-one, I came to England to study. The visit became permanent when I married a South African exile. The outrageous "Immorality Act" further prevented our return. I became a teacher, but only began writing eleven years ago. I wanted my own two children, as well as others, to ask questions. In 1991 I visited South Africa freely for the first time after twenty-six years.

Writing for me has been a way of exploring the country of my

144

childhood from the perspective of the child I was not. *Journey to Jo'burg* is the story of two children in search of their mother who works far away in the city, looking after someone else's child—unaware that her own baby is desperately ill. The journey is more than a physical one. It is a psychological one, too—for my characters, for me the author, and, hopefully, for my readers. In the sequel, *Chain of Fire*, I wanted to discover what it is like to be told that your home is to be destroyed and you are to be moved, and what it is like to try to resist.

I have still not given up teaching, even though most of my work is teaching teachers these days. I still feel angry about my own "miseducation" as a child. I have recently finished a Ph.D., researching white teenagers' responses to literature which explores issues of racism. It was fascinating as a writer to study closely the responses of readers and their various ways of seeing. None of us comes neutrally to the books we read! More important, can books help us reshape our vision?

Bibliography

Books for Young Adults

1987   *Free as I Know* (editor)
1989   *Chain of Fire*

Books for Younger Readers

1985   *Journey to Jo'burg*

Books for Adults

1985   *Censoring Reality: An Examination of Non-Fiction Books on South Africa*
1992   *Through Whose Eyes? Exploring Racism: Reader, Text and Context*

Phyllis Reynolds Naylor

PHOTO: REX NAYLOR

I was born in Anderson, Indiana, to parents who read aloud to us every night until we were teenagers. They read everything from the Bible storybook to *The Wind in the Willows* to Mark Twain, and I loved characters and plots as far back as I can remember.

The year I began seventh grade, we moved to Joliet, Illinois, which had a marvelous high school renowned for music and drama, and I was heavily involved in both. I had always spent my spare time writing little "books," but when I was sixteen, a former Sunday school teacher wrote to say that she was now editing a church paper for children. Would I like to submit a story? I did, and she sent back a check for $4.16. Thrilled, I wrote many more for her, and slowly began trying other kinds of writing.

I married right out of high school, and never had the experience of being a single woman on my own, which was a mistake, I think. The marriage was also a mistake, because five years later my brilliant husband, who was working on his Ph.D., became paranoid schizophrenic. The next three years were spent moving from place to place, looking for doctors who could help him. Because I'd only managed to get a diploma from a junior college in the meantime, it was difficult to support us. So I began doing in earnest what had been only an avocation up until then: I wrote.

By the time it was obvious that my husband was not going to get well and I had obtained a divorce, I was working on a degree in clinical psychology. But when I graduated, supporting myself by writing, I decided I wanted to write full-time, so I gave up plans to go to graduate school, and devoted myself to the work I love.

I can't imagine writing only for children, or only for adults, or writing only one type of book. I skip from a novel for adults to a picture book, to a mystery for children, and then move on, perhaps, to a serious novel for young adults.

There are parts of myself in every book I write. *The Keeper* was written because I always wondered how I would have coped with mental illness in the family if I had been a teenager at the time. *A String of Chances* deals with religious doubts I have had; *The Year of the Gopher* because I saw how often young people are pressured to get into Ivy League schools; and I wrote *Send No Blessings* because it had taken me a long time as a young girl to build up self-esteem. My "Alice" books recount some of the most embarrassing and hilarious episodes in my life as an adolescent, carefully disguised, of course, or I'd never be able to get them down on paper.

I'm married to a great guy, and we have two grown sons who are now married and parents themselves.

Bibliography

Books for Young Adults

1967	*To Shake a Shadow*
1968	*When Rivers Meet*
1970	*Making It Happen*
1972	*No Easy Circle*
1976	*Walking Through the Dark*
1980	*Shadows on the Wall* (York Trilogy, Part I)
1981	*Faces in the Water* (York Trilogy, Part II)
1981	*Footprints at the Window* (York Trilogy, Part III)
1982	*A String of Chances*
1983	*The Solomon System*
1984	*Night Cry*
1985	*The Dark of the Tunnel*
1986	*The Keeper*
1987	*The Year of the Gopher*
1990	*Send No Blessings*

Books for Middle Graders

1965	*The Galloping Goat and Other Stories,* illus. by Robert Jefferson (short stories)
1967	*What the Gulls Were Singing,* illus. by Jack Smith
1969	*To Make a Wee Moon,* illus. by Beth and Jo Krush
1971	*Wrestle the Mountain*

1973	*To Walk the Sky Path*
1975	*Witch's Sister*, illus. by Gain Owens
1976	*Getting Along with Your Family*, illus. by Rick Cooley (nonfiction)
1977	*Witch Water*, illus. by Gail Owens
1978	*The Witch Herself*, illus. by Gail Owens
1978	*How I Came to Be a Writer* (nonfiction)
1979	*Getting Along with Your Friends*, illus. by Rick Cooley (nonfiction)
1979	*How Lazy Can You Get?*, illus. by Alan Daniel
1980	*Eddie, Incorporated*, illus. by Blanche Sims
1981	*Getting Along with Your Teacher*, illus. by Rick Cooley (nonfiction)
1983	*The Mad Gasser of Bessledorf Street*
1985	*The Agony of Alice*, illus. by Blanche Sims
1986	*The Bodies in the Bessledorf Hotel*
1987	*Beetles, Lightly Toasted*, illus. by Melodye Rosales
1988	*Maudie in the Middle* (with Laura Schield Reynolds), illus. by Judith Gwyn Brown
1988	*One of the Third Grade Thonkers*, illus. by Walter Gaffney-Kessell
1989	*Alice in Rapture, Sort Of*
1990	*Bernie and the Bessledorf Ghost*
1990	*The Witch's Eye*
1991	*Shiloh*
1991	*Witch Weed*
1991	*Reluctantly Alice*
1992	*The Witch Returns*
1992	*Josie's Troubles*
1992	*All But Alice*
1993	*The Face in the Bessledorf Funeral Parlor*
1993	*The Grand Escape*
1993	*The Boys Start the War*

Books for Children

1967	*Jennifer Jean, Cross-Eyed Queen*, illus. by Harold K. Lamson
1967	*The New Schoolmaster*, illus. by Mamoru Funai
1967	*A New Year's Surprise*, illus. by Jack Endewelt
1969	*Meet Murdock*, illus. by Gioia Fiammenghi
1981	*All Because I'm Older*, illus. by Leslie Morrill
1982	*The Boy with the Helium Head*, illus. by Kay Chorao

1984	*Old Sadie and the Christmas Bear,* illus. by Patricia Mont-gomery Newton
1987	*The Baby, the Bed, and the Rose,* illus. by Mary Szilagyi
1989	*Keeping a Christmas Secret*
1991	*King of the Playground*

Short Story Collections

1965	*Grasshoppers in the Soup,* illus. by Elsa Bailey
1967	*Knee Deep in Ice Cream,* illus. by Johanna Sperl
1969	*Dark Side of the Moon*
1969	*The Private I,* illus. by Elsa Bailey
1970	*Ships in the Night*
1979	*A Change in the Wind*
1982	*Never Born a Hero*
1984	*A Triangle Has Four Sides*

Books for Adults

1977	*Crazy Love: An Autobiographical Account of Marriage and Madness* (nonfiction)
1979	*In Small Doses* (essays)
1979	*Revelations*
1986	*Unexpected Pleasures*
1989	*The Craft of Writing the Novel* (nonfiction)

Nonfiction

1972	*How to Find Your Wonderful Someone*
1974	*An Amish Family,* illus. by George Armstrong

Suzanne Newton

PHOTO: BETH SANDERS COLLEEN

Not long ago one of my daughters asked, "Did you always know you were going to be a writer?" (The question was relevant because she's taking the plunge herself.)

"Who knows?" I told her. I went on to say that when I look back, I can point out all the things that led to my being a writer here and now—the Blue-horse notebook of bad poems written in third grade; the determination, at eight or nine years of age, to write an episode for radio's "Dr. Christian" (I even sent off for the guidelines); the romantic stories written and illustrated in pencil in a hardback notebook the summer between eight and ninth grade; my love of reading; the "storyteller syndrome" (a genetic condition affecting southern people, most of whom are not writers); and so on.

But I also told her that if I had, instead, turned out to be a pianist, actress, doctor, painter, dancer, or Metropolitan Opera star (all of which I aspired to be at one time or another), I had other sets of anecdotes from my early life to show how I was inevitably heading in one of those directions. I was just extraordinarily lucky, I guess, that all the other possibilities didn't work out.

So now I say that I was always a Word Person, and I think I am telling the truth. I love making up stuff. I love guessing *why* people do what they do. I love imitating voices, attitudes, personalities. In another era I would have been a Gossip, but thank goodness I was born at a time when putting it on paper was both more satisfying and more profitable!

I was born in North Carolina and have lived somewhere in the eastern half of it all my long life. I have yet to write about any place outside of this state. Although I have lived in the city of Raleigh since 1960, most of my novels have been set in villages, rural communities, and small towns. I will never get tired of the unselfconscious lives and voices of the people who live in those places.

I am unabashed about telling people to read everything they can get their hands on, but the older I get, the less I am inclined to advise people who want to be writers. I don't think you can keep a writer from being one. Lots of people have a talent for writing, but only a small group of these can't help themselves. They *have* to write. During their growing-up years, none of my four children wanted to be writers because they had seen what writers *really* do, and as a result could not harbor the romantic notions and fantasies that often get one through the early, hard times of any venture. The daughter who asked the question was a highly paid lawyer in a big city until recently, but destiny has caught up with her, and now she is shuffling her life story to show how it couldn't have turned out any other way.

Bibliography

Books for Young Adults

1977	*What Are You Up To, William Thomas?*
1978	*Reubella and the Old Focus Home*
1981	*M. V. Sexton Speaking*
1983	*I Will Call It Georgie's Blues*
1986	*A Place Between*
1991	*Where Are You When I Need You?*

Books for Middle Graders

1971	*Purro and the Prattleberries*
1974	*C/O Arnold's Corners*
1984	*An End to Perfect*

Jean Davies Okimoto

I decided to be a writer in the sixth grade when my best friend Lola and I had a newspaper on our block in Shaker Heights, Ohio. We wrote little stories about people in the neighborhood. One of our stories offended one of our neighbors—we reported that she had dyed her hair a new color. She called my mother and complained and that was the end of *The Broxton Blab.* Although that newspaper ended, my writing didn't.

I have a theory that writers are often people who, as children, felt they weren't heard. Perhaps they develop a strong need to express themselves and tell everybody what they think and how they feel about things. I suspect it may be that drive which enables them to endure so many hours alone and so many rejection slips.

My grandfather lived with us when I was growing up and I was very close to him. He died when I was nine. In three of my novels for young people, the main character is befriended by an elderly person. Mr. Koski helped Norman in *Norman Schnurman, Average Person;* Bertha Jane Filmore helped Jason in *Jason's Women;* and Gramps helped Janie in *Take a Chance, Gramps!* I think this theme in my writing has a lot to do with my appreciation for my grandfather and my wish to re-create that relationship.

Many of the characters in my books come from diverse ethnic and racial backgrounds. It's probably a reflection of my own family; I'm Caucasian and I have two Caucasian daughters from my first marriage. My husband is Asian American and I have two Asian American stepsons. I'm sure being part of a racially mixed family influences the way I view the world and the way the world views me.

In addition to being a writer, I am also a mental health counse-

152

lor in private practice. I have a master's in psychology from Antioch University. The combination of being a writer and a psychotherapist works well for me. I can't always make the endings come out the way I'd like with the real people I see in my office; but in my writing, things always turn out nicely for my imaginary people. My husband is in the mental health field, too; he's a psychiatrist. In spite of this fact, our kids seem normal.

I had a brief experience with television when I was on a book tour for a nonfiction book I wrote for adults. I was on "The Today Show," "The Oprah Winfrey Show," CNN, and "The CBS Morning Show," as well as local TV shows all over the country. I found out I wasn't cut out for it at all. I would lose my voice and the sound transmission thing kept falling out of my ear. I decided that the only job in television I might like would be to be a staff writer for "Sesame Street."

Basically, I experience the world as a funny and sad place and I think my books pretty much reflect that.

Bibliography

Books for Young Adults

1983   *Who Did it, Jenny Lake?*
1986   *Jason's Women*
1990   *Molly By Any Other Name*

Books for Middle Graders

1979   *My Mother Is Not Married to My Father*
1980   *It's Just Too Much*
1982   *Norman Schnurman, Average Person*
1990   *Take a Chance, Gramps!*

Picture Book

1990   *Blumpoe the Grumpoe Meets Arnold the Cat*

Book for Adults

1987   *Boomerang Kids: How to Live with Adult Children Who Return Home*

Francine Pascal

I've been a New Yorker all my life. And, as far back as I can remember, a writer. At least that's what I wanted to be. My first love was poetry. I was totally captivated by one book in particular—*A Child's Garden of Verses* by Robert Louis Stevenson. His poem, "My Bed Is a Boat," was my favorite bedtime story for years. Every night I would go to sleep pretending the sea was all around me, careful to keep my hands safely on the bed so they didn't get wet.

Being a proper New Yorker, I went to New York University where I majored in journalism, but I never wrote more than one story for a newspaper. I knew very quickly that it was fiction I loved. Long before, in the sixth grade, I had gotten the poetry out of my system with a five-page original lyric poem on Ulysses that the teacher had me read to the entire class. My friends agreed it was the best nap they had had all year.

I married while I was still in college and spent the next few years raising three small daughters and writing freelance. Freelance means you're free to write and they're free not to buy it. Which is exactly what happened until 1973 when I came up with what I thought was a fabulous idea.

One night, in bed, just before sleep (my favorite time to create), I said to myself: What if a thirteen-year-old girl today couldn't get along with her mother and through some time warp went back to her mother's childhood and became her mother's best friend? (No punctuation, it all came out in one thought gush.) I loved it, and my husband, who was a columnist for *Newsday*, loved it, too.

The next day I sat down and wrote what became my first YA novel, *Hangin' Out with Cici*.

From there I went on to write three more YA novels and one

adult novel. In 1982 I created a series called Sweet Valley High. It's been my big winner—eighty-five million copies worldwide in over twenty languages—and its financial rewards have given me the freedom to go back to my first love, adult novels, and my new love, screenplays.

My mentor was my husband, John, and even though he died in 1981, the things he taught me about writing have stayed with me. Even now when I find myself spending too much time on one sentence, or one chapter, I hear him saying, "Keep going. Don't stop the flow. You can always come back on the rewrite."

And his other gem of advice, "Just keep writing." That was the best of all.

Bibliography

Books for Young Adults

1977	*Hangin' Out with Cici*
1979	*My First Love and Other Disasters*
1980	*Hand Me Down Kid*
1981	*Save Johanna!*
1985	*Love and Betrayal & Hold the Mayo!*

Series

1982	*Sweet Valley High*
1986	*Sweet Valley Twins*
1989	*Sweet Valley Kids*

Other Work

1968	Collaborated on Broadway musical, *George M!*

P. J. Petersen

PHOTO: MARIAN PETERSEN

I grew up on a prune farm six miles from the town of Geyserville, California. Living a hard, seemingly uneventful life, I longed to escape to more exciting parts of the world. Because we were too poor to travel, I did my exploring in books. I devoured the offerings of the branch library in Geyserville and read everything else I could get my hands on, from comic books to catalogs.

Loving books the way I did, it seemed natural to want to create my own. My friends dreamed of being firefighters or pilots; I wanted to be a writer. Growing older, I never wavered from this desire, although I occasionally dreamed of being a surgeon-writer or a ballplayer-writer.

I was not an immediate success. In fact, I wrote seriously for over twenty years without selling a single word—not even a greeting-card verse. I wondered why I should continue. Writing words that nobody read seemed as pointless as delivering a speech to an empty room.

Everything changed for me when I decided to write a novel for my daughter Karen, who was an eighth grader. I had never written for young people before, but I knew what kinds of books Karen enjoyed. Suddenly I had a purpose—and a reader. I wasn't optimistic about publishing the book (remember my track record), but I planned to give her the manuscript, a present from a loving father.

After numerous revisions and several title changes, that book became my first published novel, *Would You Settle for Improbable?* Since then I have written nine novels for young people. (I'm not counting the unfortunate books that died during childbirth.)

I spend about a year on each book. Before I write any words that will actually appear in the book, I generally fill a hundred pages or more with thoughts about the characters and the events.

These pages serve as a kind of outline. When the characters and the action are clear enough in my mind, I sit down and write a first draft of the novel. Once I have this rough version on paper, I go back and start to shape the work. By the time I send off a novel to a publisher, I have done about fifteen revisions. Even then, I'm never quite satisfied. Whenever I read aloud from my books, I end up changing words.

I have tried to avoid repeating myself, experimenting with different kinds of books—adventure, comedy, mystery, even fantasy. If there is a unity in my work, it is in the approach to life taken by my most sympathetic characters, the ones who keep trusting and hoping and caring, even though they've been hurt and disappointed.

My attitude about writing is continually changing. On good days, I write for hours at a stretch, totally lost in my story. On bad days, I rewrite the same paragraph thirty times, and it's still not right. On good days I have enough ideas for fifty books; on bad days, I don't think I'll ever finish the book I'm on.

But even on the worst of days, I can't imagine living without writing. It would be like living without music or poetry or sunrises. Possible maybe, but hardly worth calling life.

Bibliography

Books for Young Adults

1981   *Would You Settle for Improbable?*
1982   *Nobody Else Can Walk It for You*
1983   *The Boll Weevil Express*
1984   *Here's to the Sophomores*
1985   *Corky and the Brothers Cool*
1986   *Going for the Big One*
1987   *Goody-bye to Good Ol' Charlie*
1987   *The Freshman Detective Blues*
1988   *How Can You Hijack a Cave?*
1992   *Liars*

Books for Younger Readers

1990   *The Fireplug Is First Base*
1991   *I Hate Camping*
1992   *The Sub*

K. M. Peyton

I spent my early life in the London suburbs and went to Wimbledon High School. When I was seventeen, my family moved to Manchester and I studied art at Manchester Art School, where I met and later married a fellow student, Michael Peyton, who became a freelance designer and cartoonist. I taught art in the early years of our marriage until my husband and I started a family and settled in Essex by a river estuary.

I have written since I was a child, and I had my first book published while I was still at school (*Sabre the Horse from the Sea*). Since then I have published over thirty novels, mostly for older children, the most well-known of which is *Flambards*, which, with its sequels *The Edge of the Cloud* and *Flambards in Summer*, was made into a thirteen-part serial by Yorkshire Television in 1979. *The Edge of the Cloud* won the Library Association's Carnegie Medal in 1969 and the Flambard trilogy won the Guardian Award in 1970.

My husband and I have two daughters, now grown and living in London. We still live in an isolated house on the edge of the Essex marshes and work at writing and illustration. My main diversion is riding and anything to do with horses (I keep three and care for them myself) and my husband's is sailing and skiing. I still try to paint, and have a very large garden, wood, and fields to look after.

Bibliography

Books for Young Adults
1966   *Thunder in the Sky*
1972   *A Pattern of Roses*

1977	*Prove Yourself a Hero*
1978	*A Midsummer Night's Death*
1987	*The Right Hand Man*
1989	*Darkling*
1992	*The Boy Who Wasn't There*

Books for Younger Readers

1968	*Fly by Night*
1975	*The Team*
1983	*Who, Sir? Me, Sir?*
1988	*Downhill All the Way*

Children's Books

1984	*Going Home*
1985	*Froggett's Revenge*
1988	*Plain Jack*
1989	*Skylark*
1990	*Poor Badger*
1992	*Apple Won't Jump*

Series

The Flambards Books

1967	*Flambards*
1969	*The Edge of the Cloud*
1969	*Flambards in Summer*
1981	*Flambards Divided*

The Pennington Books

1970	*Pennington's Seventeenth Summer*
1971	*The Beethoven Medal*
1973	*Pennington's Heir*
1979	*Marion's Angels* (reissued as *Fallen Angels*)

Books for Adults

1981	*Dear Fred*
1985	*The Sound of Distant Cheering*
1990	*No Roses Round the Door*
1992	*Late to Smile*

Tamora Pierce

PHOTO: GEORGE ZARR

I grew up in a number of places, spending six years in the San Francisco Bay area and the rest in Fayette County, Pennsylvania. After my parents' divorce, we were poor—I went to the University of Pennsylvania on a full scholarship. There I studied psychology, among other things, and chose work experiences that would lead to going into social work with teenagers.

I took only one writing course (I never expected to write enough to make a living; stories were a wonderful way to escape the real world). My teacher, writer David Bradley, suggested that I write a novel. He had recommended that I base it on my life experiences, but I found that too difficult. Dramatic as my life might sound, it seemed boring (and depressing) to me when I tried to set it down on paper. Instead, I thought back to the ideas that caused me to write so much as a teenager: sword-and-sorcery fantasy, centered around a female hero. That was all I needed to start me on a career as a novelist.

I came to write for teenagers by accident. In 1977, I lived with my father and stepmother in Idaho, where I worked as a live-in housemother in a group home for teenage girls. At that time I had recently completed a novel for adults which I called *The Song of the Lioness*. My girls asked to see it, but the director of the home felt parts of it were inappropriate for them to read (it was a strict home). Instead I *told* Alanna's story, each day after school and at night before bedtime. In 1980, when my agent recommended that I turn *Song* into a four-book series for teenagers, I realized I already had—the only thing left to do was put it all on paper.

Apart from the pleasure of storytelling, I became a writer because I wanted fame and fortune. I never dreamed I would find such deep satisfaction in writing for teenagers. Readers' reactions are so passionate and vivid that I feel I have reached them at a level where they will remember for years what I say to them.

That's important to me. I write about people who cut their own deal with life, shaping their futures to fit their unique skills and outlooks. That is the approach to life that had worked for me and for those *I* respect, and from what my readers tell me in their letters, that is the point of view they take away from my books. I will try other genres, including fiction for adult readers, but I will continue to write for teenagers. I may have stumbled into this field by accident, but I plan to stay.

Advice to young writers? Write what makes you want to write more—write what's *fun*. Art, realism, and polish will come as your hands become more accustomed to translating ideas from your brain to paper. Trust me!

Bibliography

Series

The Song of the Lioness Quartet

1983   *Alanna: The First Adventure*
1984   *In the Hand of the Goddess*
1986   *The Woman Who Rides Like a Man*
1988   *Lioness Rampant*

Daine and the Immortals

1992   *Wild Magic*

Philip Pullman

I spent a lot of time on board ship when I was a boy, traveling between Africa and Australia and England, and in those days you traveled by sea. So one way or another, I saw many things and many parts of the world before I was eleven, but one thing I didn't see was TV. I'm grateful for that, I think TV is a marvelous medium, but I'm glad I grew up without it.

Instead of TV, I had books. I read, and read, and read. I'm a printoholic. Printoholics take a book with them everywhere—when they go to the cinema, for example, in case they have to wait before the movie starts; but *real* printoholics take two books, in case they finish the first one. That's me. It seemed only natural for me to become a storyteller myself; I can't remember a time when I wasn't making up stories of one sort or another.

As well as loving stories, I loved words. You don't actually need words to tell stories; you can do it with pictures, or in mime. So I might have become a comic-strip artist or an actor, except that I love the taste of words. They have a taste and a weight and a colour as well as a sound and a shape, and I enjoy making patterns with them as I write.

I used to teach. Actually, what I did mostly was watch my pupils, and listen to them. I used to watch how the kids would react to a newcomer, and how the newcomer would gradually find a group of friends; I was fascinated by the difference between girls' friendships and boys'; and I found that every class had a natural leader, who wasn't necessarily the smartest person or the strongest or the most goodlooking. Every class has a clown, too; and a group of quiet kids who do tidy work and hand it in on time; and a group of good-humoured rowdies; and an outcast. Every class has an outcast. It's an important role. I know, because I used to fill it, until I found a way of "buying" popularity by telling stories.

But I don't teach anymore. I sit in a shed at the bottom of my garden and write. I married Jude in 1970, and we have two sons, both of whom seem as if they're going to be musicians. Sometimes when I go into a school or a library to talk about my books, someone will ask me how to become a writer. There's only one way, I'm afraid, and that's hard work: write a regular amount every day. Forget about inspiration. Any fool can write when inspired. It takes a real writer to write when not. But like the golfer who found that the more he practised, the luckier he got, you'll find that the more regularly you work, the more readily inspiration comes. It's a curious world.

Bibliography

Books for Children and Young Adults

1982	*Count Karlstein*
1985	*The Ruby in the Smoke*
1986	*Shadow in the North* (in the U.K. as *The Shadow in the Plate*)
1987	*How to Be Cool*
1989	*Spring-Heeled Jack*
1990	*Frankenstein* (adapted for the stage)
1990	*The Broken Bridge*
1991	*Count Karlstein* (a version in pictures)
1991	*The Tiger in the Well*
1992	*The White Mercedes*

Stage Plays for Children

1985	*Sherlock Holmes and the Adventure of the Sumatran Devil*
1986	*The Three Musketeers*
1988	*Frankenstein*

Television Scripts

1988	*How to Be Cool* (3-part mini-series)

Ann Rinaldi

PHOTO: BART EHRENBERG

I grew up in a Revolutionary War-era house in central New Jersey, but it had no real influence on me as a historical novelist. My childhood there was unhappy. I now refer to the household as "William Faulkner East."

My mother and father (a self-made, successful man) had bought the house and the surrounding five acres just before I was born. Mother went back to New York to have me and never returned. She died. Within a year my father brought in a "housekeeper," and they were married. I'd been given to a beloved aunt and uncle in Brooklyn, in a house with teenaged cousins who adored and spoiled me. Until one day when I was about three and my father came and told my aunt to "pack the kid up" and took me to this thirteen-room house in New Jersey and into the care of this Germanic stepmother. I was not to see my Brooklyn family again until I was fourteen.

My older siblings were never allowed to mention our real mother. No trace of her was about. But I always knew something was wrong in this house. Without making this a "Mommy Dearest," let's just say my stepmother was unloving and it was a sad and emotionally deprived childhood, with too many dark undercurrents and secrets. I took refuge in books. With the outbreak of World War II, my father switched us to Catholic school, five miles away, because our school was across the street from an arsenal. And more terror came into my life.

I was terrified of the nuns, of the city kids who were all blond-haired and blue-eyed and belonged to cliques. I never belonged, I hated school, and in twelve years, all I learned to do was type and pray.

When I graduated high school, my father announced there

164

would be no college for me because all I would ever be good for was to "fill up baby bottles." I was already writing poetry and short stories, winning essay contests. I went to work at age seventeen in the typing pool and, for the next eight years, changed one office for another until I met my husband, Ron.

We married in 1960. I moved out of the thirteen-room house and never went back. Home during the '60s with two toddlers, I started writing. I wrote four novels, sent them out, accumulated piles of rejection slips. In 1968, I asked my local weekly newspaper in Somerset County for a column and got it.

In the next two years I self-syndicated my column to eighteen dailies and weeklies in the tri-state area. In 1970 I approached *The Trentonian* in Trenton. The editor, F. Gilman Spencer, hired me in five minutes to do two columns a week for the women's page. It was a lively tabloid with a newsroom bursting with talent. I fell in love with the newspaper business, started writing features and in 1975 went full-time.

For twenty-one years I was a general-interest columnist at that paper. Twice I won first place in New Jersey Press Association Awards. I went back to novel writing in 1978, wrote four contemporary young adult novels, then started doing historicals.

I'd covered many stories about the Bicentennial in historic Trenton. My son, Ron, then fourteen, joined a historic reenactment group after getting involved in the Christmas Day Crossing of the Delaware. His sister followed and, for the next eight years, my husband and I went along with them, putting on battles and encampments of the American Revolution in the thirteen original colonies.

I learned my history, hands-on, making the clothes of the eighteenth century, cooking the food, learning the songs, dances, philosophy, lifestyle. In 1981, after attending the 200th anniversary of the Battle of Yorktown, Virginia, I decided to do a YA historical. I placed it in Trenton. Ten publishers turned it down, saying they couldn't give children history. By then I had two children in college. I finally sold my first historical and publishers have been asking me for nothing else since.

I now devote myself full-time to writing historical novels and doing speaking engagements. I owe my son thanks for his influence and for his historical expertise. I also owe thanks to the field of journalism. The girl who was only good for filling baby bottles did that and then some.

Bibliography

Books for Young Adults

1980	*Term Paper*
1982	*Promises Are for Keeping*
1985	*But in the Fall I'm Leaving*
1986	*Time Enough for Drums*
1987	*The Good Side of My Heart*
1988	*The Last Silk Dress*
1991	*Wolf by the Ears*
1991	*A Ride into Morning*
1992	*A Break with Charity*
1993	*The Long Ride to McLeans*

Willo Davis Roberts

PHOTO: SAM WATTERS

I grew up in Michigan, where I learned to enjoy the outdoors. I now live in Washington State, which has not only woods and water but mountains. My family was poor, and we moved so much that I seldom stayed in one place long enough to make any friends. That's probably why I began to write. It was my way of dealing with loneliness and anxiety. Children still suffer from poverty, lack of support, fear of the future. They also need laughter, affection, and appreciation.

Many of my books are mysteries. Some of them are amusing, some are about serious things such as child abuse and having diabetes. *To Grandmother's House We Go* is about siblings who fear being put in separate foster homes.

My husband, who is also a writer, likes adventure. We've been in a rock slide in the mountains in California, were nearly washed over a cliff by a flash flood, and had a huge bear try to get into our trailer with us in Alaska. Sometimes it scares me, but it's given me wonderful material to write about. We travel to schools all over the country and talk to thousands of kids every year. Sometimes I write stories about the things they tell me of their own lives. I answer hundreds of letters from many more whom I've never met except through the pages of my books.

Some of the things in my stories are based on real events that happened to our own kids or grandchildren, and some are simply made up. I write first to entertain myself, and I find that this engages other people as well.

Although *The Girl with the Silver Eyes* is about a girl who can move things without touching them, which is certainly unusual, most of my stories are about regular kids who have extraordinary things happen to them. One girl asked me how she could write exciting stories when nothing really interesting had ever happened to her. I told her about playing the game of "what if." Imagine what would happen to a person who saw a crime committed, as Rob did in *View From the Cherry Tree*. Or if your mother disappeared, as in *Scared Stiff*. What would you do? Or perhaps you might be stranded in a strange airport, like the kids in *What Could Go Wrong?*, and you had to deal with dangerous men all by yourself. Or what if you discovered a very peculiar book, such as Alex found in *The Magic Book*, which led into some funny and spooky adventures?

I intend to go on writing more books as long as I live, or at least as long as readers will go on reading them, because it's what I enjoy most of anything. I don't think I'll ever run out of ideas. Neither will anyone who plays "what if."

Bibliography

Books for Children and Young Adults

1975   *The View From the Cherry Tree*
1977   *Don't Hurt Laurie!*
1978   *The Minden Curse*
1980   *More Minden Curses*
1980   *The Girl With the Silver Eyes*
1983   *House of Fear*
1983   *The Pet Sitting Peril*
1983   *No Monsters in the Closet*
1984   *Eddie and the Fairy Godpuppy*
1984   *Elizabeth*
1984   *Caroline*
1985   *Baby Sitting is A Dangerous Job*
1985   *Victoria*
1986   *The Magic Book*
1987   *Sugar Isn't Everything*
1988   *Megan's Island*
1989   *What Could Go Wrong?*
1989   *Nightmare*
1990   *To Grandmother's House We Go*
1991   *Scared Stiff*
1991   *Dark Secrets*
1992   *Jo and the Bandit*
1993   *What Are We Going to Do About David?*

The Black Pearl Series

1978	*The Dark Dowry*
1978	*The Cade Curse*
1978	*The Stuart Stain*
1979	*The Devil's Double*
1979	*The Radkin Revenge*
1979	*The Hellfire Heritage*
1979	*The Macomber Menace*
1980	*The Gresham Ghost*

Books for Adults

1955	*Murder at Grand Bay*
1957	*The Girl Who Wasn't There*
1961	*Murder Is So Easy*
1962	*The Suspected Four*
1966	*Nurse Kay's Conquest*
1966	*Once a Nurse*
1967	*Nurse at Mystery Villa*
1969	*Return to Darkness*
1970	*Shroud of Fog*
1970	*Devil Boy*
1970	*The Waiting Darkness*
1970	*Shadow of a Past Love*
1970	*The House at Fern Canyon*
1970	*The Tarot Spell*
1970	*Invitation to Evil*
1971	*The Terror Trap*
1971	*King's Pawn*
1971	*The Gates of Montrain*
1971	*The Watchers*
1971	*The Ghosts of Harrel*
1972	*Inherit the Darkness*
1972	*Nurse in Danger*
1972	*Becca's Child*
1972	*Sing a Dark Song*
1972	*The Nurses*
1972	*The Face of Danger*
1972	*Dangerous Legacy*
1972	*Sinister Gardens*
1972	*The M.D.*
1973	*The Evil Children*

Colby Rodowsky

I remember a time, early in the fourth grade, when our class was told to write a composition about autumn. I struggled and sighed and didn't seem to be getting anywhere when finally Sister Camille stopped at my desk, read what I had written, and gave me my first lesson in creative writing.

"You want to tell about the leaves," I remember her saying. "How they are red and yellow and orange. How they crackle underfoot and how the air smells and the sky's a special kind of blue."

For the first time, in that fourth-grade classroom, I began to understand the magic of writing. And I knew, more than anything, that I wanted to become a writer. From that time on, I wrote, filling notebooks and scraps of paper, telling myself that someday I'd be a *real* writer.

I was born in Baltimore, lived for a while in New York and Washington, D.C., came back to Baltimore, went to college, got married, taught third grade and then special education, and had six children. When the youngest child was in elementary school, I started writing again. It was then I learned that the magic of writing also involved a lot of plain hard work.

As you can imagine, my husband and I live very busy lives, with children and in-laws, and now grandchildren; with work and travel. And I've found, through the years, that the seeds of my books are all around me.

My first book, *What About Me?*, came about largely from my experiences teaching children in special education; *H, My Name is Henley* started because of a girl and her mother I watched in the park one day. A character named Slug October wandered into my head and I had to think of a story about her which led to *Evy-Ivy-*

Over, and then, years later, I wondered what Slug would be like at seventeen and if she'd ever met up with her mother again, so I wrote *Julie's Daughter.* My book *Sydney, Herself* was written because I asked myself what would happen if a teenage girl was secretly sure that her father was really a famous rock star. And *Lucy Peale* started simply because I wanted to write a love story and then, in the course of the book, I came to know Lucy, pregnant and alone, who meets Jake and learns a lot about caring—and being cared for in return.

Several of my books are set on the eastern shores of Maryland and Virginia, where I spent my childhood summers, and *The Gathering Room* takes place in an old cemetery in downtown Baltimore. *Dog Days,* the story of Sandy the Super Dog, was written in celebration of my own all-time favorite dog, a golden retriever named Sandy.

I'm often asked, "What should I do to become a writer?"

The answer to that is easy. "Read," I always say.

"Read, read, read. And read some more."

Bibliography

Books for Young Adults

1976	*What About Me?*
1980	*A Summer's Worth of Shame*
1982	*H, My Name Is Henley*
1985	*Julie's Daughter*
1989	*Sydney, Herself*
1992	*Lucy Peale*

Books for Middle Graders

1978	*P.S. Write Soon*
1978	*Evy-Ivy-Over*
1981	*The Gathering Room*
1983	*Keeping Time*
1987	*Fitchett's Folly*
1990	*Dog Days*

Books for Younger Readers

1992	*Jenny and the Grand Old Great Aunts*

Margaret I. Rostkowski

PHOTO: KENT MILES

I n the years before I began my first novel, I was preparing to write, gathering material, accumulating moments worth reconstructing on paper. All that came before is now material to think and write about: playing with my brother and sister in the foothills behind our Utah home; the parachute jump I did at age nineteen; the visits to the Catholic hospital where my father was a doctor; the music from my mother's great black piano. Not high drama, but all material that can be used as impetus or embroidery for a story.

Family stories fuel my writing: my great-uncles who were gassed and who caught measles in World War I, and my grandfather who rode a motorcycle to teach school. I don't use the exact story but the feelings. Since living with other people in families is one of the greatest challenges of life, I am drawn to write about families and the tangled threads of love, memory, and hate that bind families.

In high school, a wonderful teacher, George Taylor, taught me all the important things I needed to know about writing and teaching writing. In the years between high school and that January day when I began *After the Dancing Days*, I attended Middlebury College and the University of Kansas, married, taught school, traveled, loved all the animals and friends that entered my life. In short, I prepared to write. And now I write as often as the rest of my life allows me to do.

Teaching enriches my life and my writing. I have the best teaching assignment possible: working with high school seniors who are just about to leave for college and with a wide mix of students who want to write. My students give me ideas, models, language for characters. They also help me know which questions and issues are important at their age.

173

My books begin with questions, with things I want to explore and learn more about. *After the Dancing Days* began when I wondered what life could be for someone so badly mutilated that people turned away from him in horror. And *The Best of Friends* began when my students asked me to write about the period of the Vietnam War, a time they are curious about but find few adults willing to discuss. My next novel again revolves around the workings of a family, specifically two sisters and their mother.

I enjoy all of writing: the first excitement of falling in love with characters; the thrashing out of the plot; the revision, the hard work of finding the feeling buried beneath the surface of the moment.

In trying to write as well and as honestly as I can, I follow a few practices: I don't watch much television; I read, especially the kind of writing I hope to do; I listen and talk to other writers; I explore the land where I live; I watch live baseball; I walk with my dog every day. And always, in my head, I write.

Bibliography

Books for Young Adults

1986   *After the Dancing Days*
1989   *The Best of Friends*
1994   *Ghost Women*

Lois Ruby

It was never my dream to be known as the Pig Lady of Kansas, but somehow that title has stuck like dandruff on a black sweater. It's come about since I wrote a book called *Pig-Out Inn.* On its cover are three diabolical pigs with luminous blue eyes. People have responded to those strange creatures by showering me with pigs of every possible weird stripe. In my office, I've got stuffed pigs, pewter boars, swine wind chimes, pig pens, and a calendar that shows pigs in ordinary domestic settings, such as wallowing in mud and guzzling swill. Above my desk is a poster of a pig in a hammock. She has dozed off reading a good book, and her glasses are askew over her snout. She reminds me each day that I want to write stories which don't put people to sleep.

I read a lot when I was growing up in San Francisco before Nintendo, before shopping malls, before videos, and during those early days of TV when the screen was dark twenty hours a day. Every Saturday morning I walked to the library, reading even as I crossed the street. I ignored cars honking at me, because I was intent on finishing that last book of the week. The library was full of dark woods petrified nearly to stone in seventy-five years of wear, and in that echoey cavern I had two choices. One: I could go to the Children's Reading Room, but to do that, I had to pass a mean-looking librarian who seemed to be a branch of the tree from which her desk had sprung. Two: I could avoid her and go the other way, into the Adult Reading Room. Which would *you* choose? So that's why I never read children's books until I was in college. Once I began reading them, it was only a small leap to writing them. Along the way, I even became a librarian, despite the threatening tree branch.

Most of my books are about teenagers, because the teens I know are more interesting than adults. I can't actually say I write *for* teenagers. If kids like the stories, that's a lovely bonus, but I have to be honest: I write only for myself.

I've got the same wonderful husband I started with in 1965, and three sons who are all in college. Mostly, my sons find it amusing to have a mother who's a writer and far less embarrassing now than when I used to make "author visits" to their junior highs. Now that they're away at college, I drive to lots of schools, in my car that has all their university stickers above the bumper sticker that reads, HAVE YOU HUGGED A PIG TODAY?

The message sure fits the Pig Lady of Kansas.

Bibliography

Books for Young Adults

1977 *Arriving at A Place You've Never Left* (short stories)
1979 *What Do You Do in Quicksand?*
1982 *Two Truths in My Pocket* (short stories)
1984 *This Old Man*
1993 *Miriam's Well*

Books for Middle Graders

1987 *Pig-Out Inn*

Cynthia Rylant

I was born on an army base in Hopewell, Virginia, probably delivered by someone called "Sarge." I'm not sure. I was handed to my army father and my beautiful mother, and I spent the next four years having my diapers changed and my milk wiped up in places like Columbia, South Carolina; Peoria, Illinois; and Kyoto, Japan. I loved a little dog named Sissy, an imaginary friend named Gretchen, a toy monkey named Jo-Jo, a tiny tin sink which ran real water, and, most dearly, my two parents. But they had a disastrous marriage, an ongoing cyclone of a marriage, and when I was barely past four, my mother left everything behind me and we flew (almost literally) to a small white wooden house in Cool Ridge, West Virginia, where, finally, I found home.

The next years, until I was eight, I was raised by my coalmining grandfather and my steady grandmother and whatever other relatives happened to be living in the house at the time. It was a four-room house, no running water, no indoor plumbing at all, situated in a forsaken but stunningly beautiful part of Appalachia. Days were quiet. Birds and cowbells, the buzz of bumblebees, the baying of far-off dogs. Everything smelled good. Milk smelled good, and ripe tomatoes, bacon, and molasses. Rosebushes, honeysuckle, pine. Smoke rose from the tops of houses in winter and everyone went to church on Christmas Day. Every child got Christmas oranges and ribbon candy.

I soaked it all up, every last bit of it, everything I could take at so young an age, and when I grew up I began to ease these memories out, little by little, and I led them into books.

The date of my birth is June 6, 1954; the anniversary of D-Day, which seems fitting for a child born among soldiers. My father never recovered from being a soldier. The hepatitis he contracted in the Korean War finally killed him (with some help from liquor). The decade of my childhood, the Sixties, was also penetrated and wounded by war, this time in Vietnam. But I didn't lose anyone to Vietnam. My friends who died young died from drugs. Kids raised among honeysuckle bushes and faithful dogs, kids unprepared and unsuspicious when later, kicking about after high school, someone offered them a quick high. None of us had ever really been taught the true meaning of evil. We trusted everything.

I didn't write, growing up. I twirled a baton and went on dates and ran for student council. I didn't know, and wasn't told, to want better than just being somebody's wife. But though I planned to in fact be only that, fate said forget it, and I ended up going to college (on my late father's G.I. Bill) and majoring in English. I loved college. I loved reading Langston Hughes and James Agee. I loved the boys in flannel shirts who made pottery and smelled like patchouli. I loved the girls in the dorm who popped popcorn at 4:00 a.m. and dyed their hair green. College was one long wonderful Hollywood movie.

After college I happened into the children's room of a public library (for the first time) and, at twenty-four, I found out what I wanted to do. I wanted to write.

I did. I wrote stories and mailed them from West Virginia into the bellies of New York publishing houses. And now, thirteen years later, I have a son, some dogs and cats, a tortoise and a fish, and a huge pile of books bearing my name sitting on shelves in that same children's room in that same library. And I managed to work a few titles into the young adult section as well.

You really never know what surprises life will pull. You may think you can see yourself at twenty-five or thirty-five or sixty-five, but the universe has more imagination than you have. And it's going to surprise you.

Bibliography

Books for Young Adults

1985   *A Blue-Eyed Daisy*
1986   *A Fine White Dust*
1988   *A Kindness*
1990   *A Couple of Kooks, and Other Stories about Love*
1992   *Missing May*

Books for Children

1982 *When I Was Young in the Mountains,* illus. by Diane Goode
1983 *Miss Maggie,* illus. by Thomas di Grazia
1984 *The Year's Garden,* illus. by Mary Szilagyi
1985 *Every Living Thing,* illus. by Stephen D. Schindler
1985 *The Relatives Came,* illus. by Stephen Gammell
1986 *Night Country,* illus. by Mary Szilagyi
1987 *Birthday Presents,* illus. by Sucie Stevenson
1987 *Children of Christmas,* illus. by Stephen D. Schindler (in the U.K. as *Silver Packages and Other Stories*)
1988 *All I See,* illus. by Peter Catalonotto
1989 *Mr. Griggs' Work,* illus. by Julie Downing
1991 *Appalachia: The Voices of Sleeping Birds,* illus. by Barry Moser
1992 *An Angel for Solomon Singer,* illus. by Peter Catalonotto

Series—Henry and Mudge

1987 *Henry and Mudge*
1987 *Henry and Mudge in Puddle Trouble*
1987 *Henry and Mudge in the Green Time*
1987 *Henry and Mudge under the Yellow Moon*
1988 *Henry and Mudge and the Sparkle Days*
1989 *Henry and Mudge and the Forever Sea*
1989 *Henry and Mudge Get the Cold Shivers*
1990 *Henry and Mudge and the Happy Cat*
1991 *Henry and Mudge and the Bedtime Thumps*
1991 *Henry and Mudge Take the Big Test*
1992 *Henry and Mudge and the Long Weekend*
1992 *Henry and Mudge and the Wild Wind*
1993 *Henry and Mudge and the Careful Cousin*

Other Books

1984 *Waiting to Waltz: A Childhood,* illus. by Stephen Gammell (poetry)
1989 *But I'll Be Back Again: An Album*
1990 *Soda Jerk,* illus. by Peter Catalonotto (poetry)

Judith St. George

How old are you? How much money do you make? When did you start writing? These are the three questions that kids invariably ask me when I give talks in schools. I confess that I fudge on the first two and hurry onto the third. In 1941, when I was ten (there, I answered the first question!), I wrote a play, cast myself as the lead, enlisted my friends as actors, directed, and produced it. When our teacher, Mrs. Fish, led our class to the auditorium for the opening, and closing, performance, I knew that I was hooked, and I've been writing ever since, first diaries and letters, then school newspaper articles, college magazine stories, and, finally, books.

If kids ask three questions, adults ask only one: Are you still writing children's books? What they mean is: Haven't you graduated to writing adult books yet? It's as dumb a question as asking a pediatrician or a teacher if she or he is still working with children.

Writing children's and young adult books is what I do, what I love to do, and what I shall always do. It's a given that my writing style is appropriate for children. But more than that, the honesty and openness of children are what appeal to me as a writer. If they like your book, they tell you. If they don't like your book or don't understand it, they tell you that, too. Now that my own four children, and three grandchildren, live far away, I treasure my connections with kids when I visit their schools, though the connections are never deep, personal, or long enough.

Growing up in Westfield, New Jersey, during the Depression and World War II was a good Leave-It-To-Beaver kind of life, with an extended family of parents, brother, sister, aunts, uncles, and two sets of grandparents living nearby. I spent those moneyless, gasless years either with my nose in a book or on the playing field. As a

180

tomboy (is that word still used?), my sixth-grade triumph was to play second base on the boys' softball team.

My two years of boarding school were an unhappy time. But college was glorious, as were two subsequent years of working at a fun job, followed, in turn, by my marriage to David St. George, a fledgling Episcopal minister. We moved from the East coast to the West and back again, raising three boys and a girl in the process. Now that David is retired, we wonder where all those years have gone.

Although I have switched between historical fiction, mysteries, and nonfiction, no matter what genre I tackle, I somehow find myself in my books. I was a timid child who leapt from my doorway into bed so that whatever was under the bed couldn't grab my ankles. I'm a worrier. I care about, and work at, my friendships. Sports have always been important to me. David and I love to travel. American history fascinates me, as do larger-than-life people who overcome great odds to achieve their dreams. All these disparate elements that make up my *persona* underlie my books, and although I never set out to write about myself, in the end, no writer can divorce the kind of person she or he is from their works, and I guess that I am no exception.

Bibliography

Fiction for Young Adults
1970   *Turncoat Winter, Rebel Spring*
1975   *The Girl with Spunk*
1976   *The Chinese Puzzle of Shag Island*
1977   *The Shadow of the Shaman*
1978   *The Halo Wind*
1979   *Mystery at St. Martin's*
1980   *Haunted*
1981   *Call Me Margo*
1982   *Do You See What I See?*
1983   *In the Shadow of the Bear*
1986   *What's Happening to My Junior Year?*
1987   *Who's Scared? Not Me!*

Fiction for Younger Readers
1976   *By George, Bloomers!*
1977   *The Shad are Running*

1978   *The Halloween Pumpkin Smasher*
1981   *The Mysterious Girl in the Garden*

Nonfiction
1980   *The Amazing Voyage of the New Orleans*
1982   *The Brooklyn Bridge: They Said It Couldn't Be Built*
1985   *The Mount Rushmore Story*
1989   *Panama Canal: Gateway to the World*
1990   *The White House: Cornerstone of a Nation*
1991   *Mason and Dixon's Line of Fire*
1992   *Dear Dr. Bell . . . Your Friend, Helen Keller*

Otto R. Salassi

I was born in 1939, in Vicksburg, Mississippi, and lived in the best time and place I think this century had to offer. It's true we had WWII and I had a brother fighting in it, but I didn't know my brother, since I was only two when he went off to fight. All I knew was that we had a blue star in the window, some great war movies to go see, and a party I'll never forget when he and his buddies all came home.

Adults were so busy and there was such little crime that kids my age were allowed to run free, and run free we did. We had a trolley line to ride out to the swimming pool and ballpark. We had a team in the Southeastern League called the "'Billies," a great library, and an even greater bunch of parks and playgrounds where we met to play unsupervised games. It was before "organized" sports, like Little League, and anybody who's played them knows "catch-up" games were the best. Nobody broke up fistfights.

For romance and dreaming I had the river and the boats passing up and down. I had the railroads, busy with trains up to Memphis and down to New Orleans. And best of all, I had the Civil War all around me in the battlefield and in the historic houses on every city block in town.

I grew up poor, my family having lost everything during the Great Depression, but being poor wasn't so bad then as it is now. There were too many of us to make ourselves feel bad.

And I was lucky because my family was a family of readers. My father and mother and all seven of us kids read books, novels, magazines, everything. We also saw every movie that ever came to town and listened to the radio late into the night. I grew up knowing the words to every cowboy, hillbilly, rock and roll, spiritual, and standard chart song ever recorded. I also listened to every radio show from Arthur Godfrey in the morning to "The Mysterious Traveler," "The Shadow," and "Intersanctum" late at night.

In school, from the seventh to the twelfth grade, every student had to stand in front of the English class and recite 300 lines of poetry a year from memory; most of the 1,800 lines I still remember.

My first job for money was in 1947 in the local poolhall where I walked along a ramp and chalked in sports scores as they came across the wire. Other jobs I had growing up included collecting for bingo games, carhopping at a drive-in, delivering papers, clerking in a grocery store, and lifeguarding.

When I was fourteen I spent a year in Memphis living with my brother, met Elvis, who knew me by name when he lived in the housing project and I lived around the corner, and in September 1954, just before my fifteenth birthday, I lied about my age and joined the Tennessee National Guard. I learned to drive a jeep, a truck, and a tank, got to fire an army Colt .45, a .30 carbine, an M-1, both .30 caliber and .50 caliber machine guns, a bazooka, a flame-thrower, and 105 and 155 mm howitzers. Before I was out of school I got promoted all the way up to sergeant and got to put my shop teacher on KP.

In high school I fell in love twice with two beautiful girls, not at the same time, but one year apart, and would have happily signed away my life to the Devil to exchange my virginity for theirs; toward that wondrous goal I devoted most of my junior and senior year's time and energy. It was, however, not to be.

Such were my life and times. If you had told me back when I was growing up how lucky I was, I would have called you crazy, which is what my kids used to call me when I told them how lucky they were, because they were living in the very best of times this century had to offer. No matter who you are or when you live, the time and place you grow up are the happiest because they are called "youth."

Looking back on it now, it's easy to see how I came to be a writer of young adult fiction. How could I not be?

Bibliography

Books for Young Adults

1981 *On the Ropes*
1984 *And Nobody Knew They Were There*
1987 *Jimmy D. Sidewinder, and Me*

Pamela Sargent

PHOTO: © JERRY BAUER

I was born in Ithaca, New York, and studied philosophy, ancient history, and Greek at the State University of New York at Binghamton, where I earned a B.A. and an M.A. I've worked as a model, salesclerk, solderer on an assembly line, typist in a library, file clerk, receptionist, and taught introductory philosophy classes at SUNY at Binghamton.

None of this will tell anyone how I became a writer.

I grew up with books in the house. My parents encouraged reading, and I picked up this skill well before starting school because my mother read to me. But, along with almost every other American child during the '50s, I also grew up with a television set. It was extreme nearsightedness that probably saved me from becoming a tube addict; I couldn't see the flickering black-and-white images on our RCA Victor all that clearly and was in second grade before anyone thought of getting my eyes checked. By then, reading was my favorite recreation, since I could hold a book close to my eyes. Glasses opened another world to me, but I was still drawn to the one that books had already revealed.

I didn't do well in school. Daydreams kept distracting me, and much of what was taught bored me; a speech defect made me hesitate to say anything in class. Only my obvious interest in books and an ability to write kept my teachers from considering me hopeless. Family problems and a growing feeling of worthlessness soon had me convinced that I was going nowhere fast. I ran away from home, got into trouble, cut school a lot, and hung around with people who were also going nowhere fast. At fourteen, I ended up in an institution with a lot of other troubled kids. One of my closest friends there had already done time in a couple of reform schools; another ended up in prison a year and half later.

185

Certainly my life would have taken a different turn after that if, after a few months, I hadn't been able to go to a good school where some very fine teachers encouraged me. I was also ready to work a lot harder at my studies instead of just goofing off. But my newfound determination and the best teachers in the world probably wouldn't have done me much good if I hadn't already loved reading and had not developed my writing ability. Those skills made up for a lot of deficits in my background and eventually helped me win a college scholarship.

Perhaps one of the reasons I write is because books were a lifeline for me; often I feel as though I'm writing for the girl I was. My hope is that the stories I tell may touch others struggling with a difficult passage to adulthood in a world much more troubled than the one I experienced.

Bibliography

Books for Young Adults

1980   *Watchstar*
1983   *Earthseed*
1984   *Eye of the Comet*
1984   *Homesmind*
1988   *Alien Child*

Books for Adults

1975   *Women of Wonder* (editor)
1976   *Cloned Lives*
1976   *Bio-Futures* (editor)
1976   *More Women of Wonder* (editor)
1977   *Starshadows* (short stories)
1978   *The New Women of Wonder* (editor)
1979   *The Sudden Star*
1982   *The Golden Space*
1983   *The Alien Upstairs*
1986   *Venus of Dreams*
1986   *Afterlives* (editor, with Ian Watson)
1986   *The Shore of Women*
1987   *The Best of Pamela Sargent* (short stories)
1988   *Venus of Shadows*
1992   *Ruler of the Sky*

Marjorie Weinman Sharmat

MARJORIE WEINMAN SHRMAT AND DUDLEY
PHOTO: MITCHELL SHARMAT

I'm writing this autobiographical sketch on a flight between Arizona and New York. This might seem to be a gratuitous bit of information, but it's actually a reflection of my *modus operandi*. Dentists' waiting rooms, doctors' waiting rooms, lines at the bank, lines at the supermarket (unless I opt to go back for the forgotten ketchup and dog food), bus stops, airplane trips . . . all translate into gifts of time and opportunity to write.

I've been writing since my early childhood in Portland, Maine. When I was growing up, I lived at 133 Dartmouth Street in Portland. One of my *Nate the Great* books is dedicated to the house there. That's where I became a reader and developed my love of books. I remember sitting and reading in a big chair in our sunroom, especially in the summer. My mother would open the window by my chair so the breeze could come in, and she'd make lemonade and bring it to me in a pink cut-glass pitcher. My sister Rosalind still has that pitcher in her apartment in New York. (I'm on my way to visit Rosalind as I write this.)

Rosalind also has the bookcase that was in the sunroom. It contained some of my favorite childhood books . . . *Black Beauty, An Old-Fashioned Girl,* and assorted mysteries. Today that bookcase is filled with books *I* wrote, and many of them were inspired by my family's names and experiences. Rosalind can go to the bookcase and pull out *A Visit With Rosalind.* Or the *Nate the Great* books, named for our father Nathan. Or *Chasing After Annie,* named for our mother, Anna. And books named for my husband Mitchell and our two sons, Craig and Andrew, and our dogs Fritz, Melvin, and Dudley.

After many years of writing for young and middle grade read-

187

ers, I created my first young adult book, *I Saw Him First*, and novelized a CBS-TV sitcom for the same age group. In my YA novels, I usually don't engage in "grand" themes. I prefer to explore a potpourri of feelings, people, and events. How we connect, how we miss. I write about people who show up, stick around, or pass from view... who hurt us, charm us, inspire us, love us, confuse us, elevate us. I write about the temporary people and the permanent people. I deal with problems that get solved or are not solvable but simply get managed. I hope that readers complete my books with a feeling of optimism. If you haven't laughed, haven't felt the comfort of knowing that your problems are not unique, I have failed.

I've now had over 100 books published. Unfortunately my mailbox is overstuffed with letters resulting from all these books, and I am as overwhelmed as my mailbox, and can no longer respond. But I'm happy for this chance to check in and say hello to all of you who love books as much as I do.

Bibliography

Books for Young Adults

1982   *Square Pegs* (TV novelization)
1983   *I Saw Him First*
1983   *How to Meet a Gorgeous Guy*
1984   *How to Meet a Gorgeous Girl*
1984   *He Noticed I'm Alive ... And Other Hopeful Signs*
1984   *Vacation Fever!* (as Wendy Andrews)
1984   *Supergirl* (movie novelization) (as Wendy Andrews)
1985   *Two Guys Noticed Me ... And Other Miracles*
1985   *Are We There Yet?* (as Wendy Andrews)
1985   *How to Have a Gorgeous Wedding*

Books for Middle Graders

1971   *51 Sycamore Lane*
1971   *Getting Something on Maggie Marmelstein*
1972   *A Visit with Rosalind*
1975   *Maggie Marmelstein for President*
1976   *The Lancelot Closes at Five*
1982   *Mysteriously Yours, Maggie Marmelstein*
1983   *Rich Mitch*

| 1985 | *Get Rich, Mitch!* |
| 1985 | *The Son of the Slime Who Ate Cleveland* |

Books for Younger Readers

1967	*Rex*
1969	*Goodnight Andrew, Goodnight Craig*
1970	*Gladys Told Me to Meet Her Here*
1971	*A Hot Thirsty Day*
1972	*Nate the Great*
1973	*Sophie and Gussie*
1973	*Morris Brookside, A Dog*
1974	*Morris Brookside Is Missing*
1974	*Nate the Great Goes Undercover*
1974	*I Want Mama*
1975	*Walter the Wolf*
1975	*I'm Not Oscar's Friend Anymore*
1975	*Nate the Great and the Lost List*
1975	*Burton and Dudley*
1976	*The Trip and Other Sophie and Gussie Stories*
1976	*Mooch the Messy*
1977	*Edgemont*
1977	*I'm Terrific*
1977	*I Don't Care*
1977	*Nate the Great and the Phony Clue*
1978	*A Big Fat Enormous Lie*
1978	*Nate the Great and the Sticky Case*
1978	*Thornton the Worrier*
1978	*Mitchell Is Moving*
1979	*Mooch the Messy Meets Prudence the Neat*
1979	*Scarlet Monster Lives Here*
1979	*Mr. Jameson and Mr. Phillips*
1979	*The 329th Friend*
1979	*I Am Not a Pest* (with Mitchell Sharmat)
1979	*Uncle Boris and Maude*
1979	*Octavia Told Me a Secret*
1979	*Say Hello, Vanessa*
1979	*Griselda's New Year*
1979	*The Trolls of 12th Street*
1980	*Little Devil Gets Sick*
1980	*What Are We Going to Do about Andrew?*
1980	*Taking Care of Melvin*
1980	*Sometimes Mama and Papa Fight*

1980	*The Day I Was Born* (with Mitchell Sharmat)
1980	*Grumley the Grouch*
1980	*Gila Monsters Meet You at the Airport*
1981	*Nate the Great and the Missing Key*
1981	*Twitchell the Wishful*
1981	*Rollo and Juliet, Forever!*
1981	*The Sign*
1981	*Lucretia the Unbearable*
1982	*The Best Valentine in the World*
1982	*Two Ghosts on a Bench*
1982	*Nate the Great and the Snowy Trail*
1983	*Frizzy the Fearful*
1984	*The Story of Bentley Beaver*
1984	*Bartholomew the Bossy*
1984	*Sasha the Silly*
1984	*My Mother Never Listens to Me*
1985	*Atilla the Angry*
1985	*Nate the Great and the Fishy Prize*
1985	*One Terrific Thanksgiving*
1986	*Hooray for Mother's Day!*
1986	*Who's Afraid of Ernestine?*
1986	*Nate the Great Stalks Stupidweed*
1987	*Helga High-Up*
1987	*Hooray for Father's Day!*
1987	*Nate the Great and the Boring Beach Bag*
1988	*Go to Sleep, Nicholas Joe*
1989	*Nate the Great Goes Down in the Dumps*
1989	*Nate the Great and the Halloween Hunt*
1990	*Nate the Great and the Musical Note* (with Craig Sharmat)
1990	*I'm Santa Claus and I'm Famous*
1991	*I'm the Best!*
1992	*Nate the Great and the Stolen Bus*

Story Books

1981	*Chasing After Annie*

Series

Marjorie Sharmat's Sorority Sisters

1986	*For Members Only*
1986	*Sobs, Beware*
1986	*I Think I'm Falling in Love*

1986   *Fighting Over Me*
1987   *Nobody Knows How Scared I Am*
1987   *Here Comes Mr. Right*
1987   *Getting Closer*
1987   *I'm Going to Get Your Boyfriend*

The Kids on the Bus (with Andrew Sharmat)

1990   *School Bus Cat*
1991   *The Cooking Class*
1991   *The Bully on the Bus*
1991   *The Secret Notebook*
1991   *The Field Day Mix-Up*
1991   *The Haunted Bus*

Olivia Sharp, Agent for Secrets (with Mitchell Sharmat)

1989   *The Pizza Monster*
1989   *The Princess of the Fillmore Street School*
1990   *The Sly Spy*
1990   *The Green Toenails Gang*

Jan Slepian

I t seems to me that what has shaped my life is largely chance, happenstance, sheer accident all the way, and I've been lucky all my life.

I'm a New Yorker, born in Manhattan and raised in Brooklyn a few blocks from the ocean in Brighton Beach. Growing up within sight and sound of the sea, it is no wonder, I suppose, that the setting of each of my books—so far—contains some body of water.

I was trained as a clinical psychologist, but when I left graduate school at the University of Washington in Seattle jobs were hard to find. I had minored in speech pathology, so when I was offered a job as language therapist at the Massachusetts General Hospital in Boston I was glad to have it. That's maybe the luckiest thing that ever happened to me because it was there that I met my husband, David. We were married in Paris and settled in New Jersey where David worked as a mathematician at Bell Labs, and I worked, too, as mother of three children full-time and speech therapist part-time.

The writer part happened when a colleague suggested we collaborate on a series of newspaper articles about everyday speech problems for worried parents. This worked out well, the articles were syndicated, and so we went on to write and publish a series of picture books, called the Listen-Hear books, all dealing with some aspect of speech. There were eleven of these in all, of which *The Hungry Thing* and *The Cat Who Wore a Pot on Her Head* are still out there, going strong.

Perhaps I would still be writing picture books exclusively if I hadn't happened to take a class in children's literature at the University of California in Berkeley. For years and years we (my family) had the odd arrangement and great good fortune to live alternately in Hawaii and New Jersey. One year we'd be bundled up in the East; the next, in the tropics, going barefoot. On our way to Hawaii in 1979, we stopped for a semester at Berkeley where my husband was guest professor. I thought the course I elected to take was about picture books. Instead I was introduced to a marvelous new (to me) genre that just didn't exist when I was growing up and reading everything in sight. The genre was teenage novels, books for older readers. It gave me the form (and the nerve) to tackle a subject that had been in the back of my mind for ages, a book about my brother Alfred. That is how my first novel, *The Alfred Summer,* came about, and how my everyday joy and struggle and addiction began.

Eight novels later I know there are bits and pieces of my life in all my books, my experiences, my concerns, and above all my feelings. No matter how disguised, in a certain sense, novel writing is autobiographical.

Bibliography

Books for Young Adults
1980   *The Alfred Summer*
1981   *Lester's Turn*
1983   *The Night of the Bozos*
1985   *Getting on with It*
1987   *Something Beyond Paradise*

Books for Middle Graders
1989   *The Broccoli Tapes*
1990   *Risk N' Roses*
1993   *Back to Before*

Picture Books
1964   Listen-Hear series

   Magic Arthur and the Giant
   The Cock Who Couldn't Crow
   Mr. Sipple and the Naughty Princess
   Alfie and the Dream Machine
   The Roaring Dragon of Redrose

1967   The Junior Listen-Hear series
   The Silly Listening Book

An Ear Is to Hear
Bendemolena
The Hungry Thing
Ding-Dong, Bing-Bong

1967   *The Best Invention of All*
1971   *The Hungry Thing* (reprinted from Junior Listen-Hear series)
1974   *The Cat Who Wore a Pot on Her Head* (originally *Bendemo-lena*)
1989   *The Hungry Thing Returns*
1992   *The Hungry Thing Goes to a Restaurant*
1993   *The Christmas Moose*
1994   *Emily Just in Time*

Gary Soto

PHOTO: CAROLYN SOTO

I spent the first six years of my life in the industrial side of Fresno. To the left of our house was a junkyard and a small business that made some sort of stationery. Across the street stood a Coleman Pickle factory, where we could fish out pickles; the owner, Mr. Coleman, didn't seem to mind. Only a few months ago I received a letter from him that started, "So that was you I saw in the barrels." Down the alley we could make out the *whack-whack* of a broom factory. And not more than two blocks away stood Sun-Maid Raisin, where my family—grandfather and grandmother, father, uncles—worked with their friends. My mother worked for Redi-Spuds. That was around the corner, not too far from Beacon Storage, a landmark building eight stories tall. I loved this area, which by the early 1960s was gutted and leveled in the name of urban renewal, a federal program that attempted to revitalize poor communities with industry. It didn't work in our area. It didn't work anywhere. The houses were bulldozed, and in their place grew weeds.

I suppose I became a writer because we were displaced by urban renewal, and my father died two months after we had left our old neighborhood. The feeling of loss was so acute that for years I had honest-to-goodness dreams of building that area back to its former glory. I remember one dream where I was on top of the roof, renailing the shingles. You would have to wonder what Freud might have thought about such a dream. The glory for me was the sense of family and place, and the utter sense of a summery freedom. I don't know where I can find this again. It's not here, in Berkeley, where our house is a pleasant house that overlooks a stand of eucalyptus. It's not San Francisco, where I once lived with my wife and daughter, and it's not the better parts of Fresno, where I sometimes drive looking for a home.

I studied at Fresno State University, where I graduated in 1974, and earned a Master of Fine Arts from the University of California at Irvine. I have written poetry and prose for adults, and the same for young people. On most days, I like what I do. It's a clean yet terrifying job. And I mean "clean" because I don't have to stuff my body in work clothes, and "terrifying" because I have to continuously scratch at experience for subjects and the imagination that will make the subjects live. I enjoy reading and eating. I enjoy traveling only if at the end of the day I can fall into bed with clean sheets.

Bibliography

Books for Young Adults

1990   *Baseball in April* (short stories)
1991   *A Fire in My Hands* (poems)
1991   *Taking Sides*
1992   *Neighborhood Odes* (poems)
1992   *Pacific Crossing*
1993   *Local News* (short stories)

Books for Younger Readers

1992   *The Ring*
1992   *The Skirt*
1993   *The Mustache*

Books for Adults

1977   *The Elements of San Joaquin*
1978   *The Tale of Sunlight*
1981   *Where Sparrows Work Hard*
1985   *Black Hair*
1985   *Living Up the Street*
1986   *Small Faces*
1988   *Lesser Evils*
1988   *California Childhood*
1990   *Who Will Know Us?*
1990   *A Summer Life*
1991   *Home Course in Religion*

Films for Children

1991   *The Bike*
1992   *The Pool Party*

Ivan Southall

PHOTO: IVAN SOUTHALL AND TAKI, 1990

Why do I write as I do? Heaven may be the only authority fully informed. As I see it, it's the way I think and feel about young people who put body, mind, and heart *on the line* as they open doors, hesitantly, on the grown-up world.

I'm drawn to my subject because life is then lived at a level that rarely comes again. That's not to imply that life ends when youth is left behind. Life begins again, but differently.

There was a period, not surprisingly, when I wrote of physical adventure. I had been a flier putting my life *on the line* almost every day. I had to write it out of my system. Now I'm attracted to adventures of another kind.

Since humans set out to conquer the earth, the sea, the sky, and the mystery of themselves, the exhilaration of adventure in the field and in the mind has attracted great spirits and their followers. Our myths, religions, legends, and histories have been built upon their deeds and discoveries.

In parallel has grown a long line of storytellers to relate the tales, each attracting his or her own share of listeners, viewers, or readers who are able to tune in on the appropriate wavelength. If the storyteller's style appears to be garbled or off-frequency to half the people on the planet, it may be exactly right for you.

I was born in Melbourne, Australia, in 1921, eldest son of parents whose lives centered on the church: my mother, an organist since childhood, my father, a parson whose career was cut short due to ill health before his marriage.

From an early age, I set out to be a writer, encouraged by my father, but in 1935 he again became seriously ill and my boyhood and schooldays were over. Partway through year nine I had to take a full-time job, six days a week, to help support the family. Before the year was out my beautiful father died and my hopes of an education equal to the needs of a writer were not looking good.

So began my personal adventures of mind and emotion. I wrote anyway, learned from my mistakes, and discovered within a year or two that newspapers and magazines were publishing my stories. World War II came. I wanted to hide under the bed, but in time resolved to be a pilot. If I could write without an appropriate education, I could fly without one. I could grit it through. And I discovered, in the same way, that I was able to. After the war, with a young family of my own to support on no money and few resources, I set out to write full-time. Again, I discovered that I could.

Bibliography

Books for Young Adults

1969	*Finn's Folly*
1971	*Josh*
1973	*Seventeen Seconds* (nonfiction)
1974	*Fly West* (nonfiction)
1977	*What about Tomorrow*
1981	*The Golden Goose*
1983	*The Long Night Watch*
1986	*Rachel*
1988	*Blackbird*
1990	*The Mysterious World of Marcus Leadbeater*

Books for Younger Readers

1950–1961	The Simon Black series (nine titles)
1962	*Hills End*
1965	*Ash Road*
1967	*The Fox Hole*
1967	*To the Wild Sky*
1967	*The Sword of Esau*
1968	*Let the Balloon Go*
1968	*The Curse of Cain*
1970	*Chinaman's Reef Is Ours*
1970	*Walk a Mile and Get Nowhere* (in the U.K. as *Bread and Honey*)
1972	*Head in the Clouds*

1972   *Benson Boy* (in the U.K. as *Over the Top*)
1973   *Matt and Jo*
1979   *King of the Stick*
1984   *A City out of Sight*
1985   *Christmas in the Tree*

Picture Book

1968   *Sly Old Wardrobe*, illus. by Ted Greenwood

Nonfiction for Younger Readers

1961   *Journey into Mystery*
1964   *Rockets in the Desert*
1964   *Lawrence Hargrave*
1965   *Indonesian Journey*
1968   *Bushfire* (survival handbook)

Books for Adults

1942   *Out of the Dawn* (short stories)
1950   *The Weaver from Meltham*
1956   *The Story of the Hermitage*
1956   *They Shall Not Pass Unseen*
1957   *A Tale of Box Hill*
1958   *Bluey Truscott*
1959   *The Third Pilot*
1959   *Flight to Gibralter*
1959   *Mediterranean Black*
1959   *Sortie in Cyrenaica*
1960   *Mission to Greece*
1960   *Atlantic Pursuit*
1960   *Softly Tread the Brave*
1962   *Woomera*
1962   *Parson on the Track*
1964   *Indonesia Face to Face*
1966   *The Challenge* (editor)
1976   *A Journey of Discovery*

Elizabeth George Speare

There is one piece of advice that is often given, especially to young writers, and that is that one should write about what one knows best. If you live in a small town in America, they say, do not try to write about London or Paris, or a desert or a mountain peak that you have never seen. But suppose, like me, that is exactly what you want to do? I have to admit that I have never been able to follow this wise advice. I wanted to write about the early days in colonial New England, or even about Palestine in the days of Jesus. And I found the answer. It is RESEARCH, a word that sounds forbidding to many people who have never discovered the fun and excitement of it. There are men and women who have lived in London or Paris or in the desert and have climbed the highest mountain peaks, and they have written books to share their experiences with stay-at-homes like me. In a library, their many worlds are waiting to be entered. Their books can tell me all about the place I have chosen—how it looks or how it looked in some former time, its history, its weather, its very smell and feel. They can show me the people who have lived there, how they dressed, what they ate, how they worked and played, and what they thought and dreamed about. Sooner or later I come to feel that I know this faraway place and that I can move about in it as confidently as in my own kitchen. My imaginary people are at home there. And I myself have had the experience of stepping into another time and place. All this is research, and it is never dull. In fact, writing historical fiction is rather like living a double life.

So you can understand why I must disagree with another saying. Writing, they say, is a lonely profession. I have never found it to be so. To be sure, I have sat for many long hours in a quiet room staring at a typewriter. (I wrote my first novel with a pencil on yellow paper at the dining room table.) But it was not lonely. The room was filled with people, young and old, happy and sad, gentle and angry, all clamoring to be heard, all with something urgent to say. Sometimes I could hear their voices clearly and could only listen to the stories they had to tell. At other times the voices were dim and far away, a hint, perhaps, that I should visit the library again. Often, when the voices were interrupted, when the telephone or the doorbell rang or some household task demanded attention, it was with reluctance that I left these imaginary people who had become, as the days went by, almost as real as my own family. Often they refused to be left behind; they followed me about, still talking, no matter what else I might be doing.

No, writing is not lonely. It is a profession crowded with life and sound and color. I feel privileged to have had a share in it.

Bibliography

Books for Young Adults
1957   *Calico Captive*
1958   *The Witch of Blackbird Pond*
1961   *The Bronze Bow*
1963   *Life in Colonial America*
1983   *The Sign of the Beaver*

Books for Adults
1967   *The Prospering*

R. L. Stine

PHOTO: MATT STINE

Q: What do you get when you cross a dog with a frog?
A: A dog that can lick himself from across the room.

I think that's one of the best jokes I've ever written. At least it made me laugh a lot when I thought of it. I wrote it a few years ago for a book of dog jokes. And, since I've become "Mr. Horror" and don't get a chance to write many joke books these days, I thought I'd slip it in here.

Someone once called me "the Jekyll and Hyde" of children's books, and I guess that's about right. I've written thirty or forty joke books and humor books for young people as Jovial Bob Stine. For ten years, in my jovial guise, I was editor of a humor magazine called *Bananas*.

These days I mostly slip into my more frightening identity as R. L. (Robert Lawrence) Stine, turning out thrillers and horror novels for young readers. So far, I've written nearly three dozen of these novels—including two series, Fear Street and Goosebumps.

I enjoy writing both kinds of books. I think the things I like best about being a writer are: (1) You don't need to do any warm-up exercises before starting, and (2) You don't need any special kind of shoes to do it.

I was born on October 8, 1943, in Columbus, Ohio. When I was nine years old, I found an old typewriter in the attic. I brought it downstairs and started typing up stories and little joke magazines. I've been writing ever since. In fact, I think I'm probably still using some of the same jokes!

I started writing novels when I was in high school. In college (Ohio State University), I was editor of the humor magazine for three years. After graduating, I moved to New York and began to search for writing jobs. I've been very lucky. I've always been able to make a living by writing. I've never had to get a *real* job!

These days, I'm concentrating on frightening as many readers as I can. I get wonderful mail from my readers—more than a hundred letters a week—and most of them ask the same question: "Where do you get your ideas?"

Unfortunately, I never had a satisfying answer to that question. Writing as many novels as I do, I really have no choice—I *have* to have ideas! I usually just sit down at my desk and don't get up until I have one. Not an interesting answer, I'll admit.

Sometimes I get lucky. A few summers ago, I decided I'd like to try writing a series of scary novels. "What could I call it?" I wondered. I sat down and started to think of a title for the series—and the words Fear Street just *popped* into my head. I didn't even have to think about it. There it was. I took the rest of the day off.

The other question I'm most asked is: Did any of the things in your scary novels ever happen to you in real life? Once again, I'm afraid the answer is disappointing. No, I've never been terrorized by a maniac, haunted by a ghost from the future, or bitten by a vampire. Once, I got a very bad paper cut. But that's about the most horrifying thing—thank goodness!—that's happened to me as a writer.

Bibliography

Books for Young Adults

1982   *The Time Raider*
1983   *Golden Sword of Dragonwalk*
1984   *Indiana Jones and the Curse of Horror Island*
1985   *Badlands of Hark*
1985   *Invaders of Hark*
1986   *Blind Date*
1987   *Twisted*
1989   *The Baby-Sitter*
1990   *Beach Party*
1990   *The Boyfriend*
1990   *How I Broke Up with Ernie*
1990   *Phone Calls*
1991   *The Snowman*
1991   *Baby-Sitter II*
1991   *The Girlfriend*

1991	*Curtains*
1991	*Broken Date*
1992	*Hit and Run*
1992	*The Beach House*
1992	*The Hitch-Hiker*

Fear Street series

1989	*The New Girl*
1989	*The Surprise Party*
1989	*The Overnight*
1990	*Missing*
1990	*The Wrong Number*
1990	*Haunted*
1990	*The Halloween Party*
1990	*The Stepsister*
1991	*Ski Weekend*
1991	*The Fire Game*
1991	*Lights Out*
1991	*The Secret Bedroom*
1992	*The Knife*
1992	*The Prom Queen*
1992	*First Date*
1992	*The Cheerleaders* (a 3-book mini-series)

Fear Street Super Chillers series

1991	*Party Summer*
1991	*Silent Night*
1992	*Goodnight Kiss*

Goosebumps series

1992	*Welcome to Dead House*
1992	*Stay out of the Basement*
1992	*Monster Blood*

As Jovial Bob Stine

Books for Young Adults

1978	*How to Be Funny*
1980	*The Sick of Being Sick Book* (with Jane Stine)
1980	*The Pigs' Book of World Records*
1981	*Gnasty Gnomes*

1981   *The Cool Kids' Guide to Summer Camp* (with Jane Stine)
1981   *The Beast Handbook*
1982   *Don't Stand in the Soup*
1982   *Bored with Being Bored* (with Jane Stine)
1982   *Blips*
1986   *101 Monster Jokes*
1987   *Spaceballs: The Book*

Books for Younger Readers

1990   *The Amazing Adventure of Me, Myself, & I*
1991   *Son of Furry*

Picture Books

1986   *Miami Mice*
1989   *Pork & Beans' Play Date*

Joyce Sweeney

I was born and raised in Dayton, Ohio, and attended Wright State University, where I graduated summa cum laude. Last year I was chosen for the Alumni of the Year Award. I did graduate work in English and creative writing at Ohio University in Athens, Ohio, where I studied under the likes of Daniel Keyes and the late Walter Tevis. After graduation, I returned to Dayton and married Jay Sweeney, who is now my husband of twelve years, and tried to make a living in advertising. This was a period of great discontent in my life. I had set my sights on being a fiction writer and had even sold several short stories to magazines (including *Playgirl* and *New Writers*) and I was not happy in the conventional workplace.

My husband persuaded me to take several years off for a full-time writing effort. The effort paid off. I found an agent, Marcia Amesterdam, and completed the novel *Center Line* which won the First Annual Delacorte Press Prize for an Outstanding Young Adult Novel. *Center Line* was also an American Library Association best book and made me a nice income in movie options. So, of course, I was hooked.

The next several years I spent living in different cities. Jay and I moved to Ormond Beach, Florida, then to Atlanta, and now we make our home just outside of Fort Lauderdale. I have been working steadily and have published three other novels for young adults, all with Delacorte, and have two more that are sold and scheduled for publication in 1992 and 1993. To pick up extra cash, I have dabbled in book reviewing, both for the *Fort Lauderdale Sun-Sentinal* and the *Atlanta Constitution*. I have also written columns and feature articles for the *Sun-Sentinal*. I teach workshops in writing on a regular basis and am currently working as a part-time book editor. I am

207

active in a writer's networking group called the Book Group of South Florida.

My principal hobbies are spending money and talking on the phone, both of which, I think, enable me to relate well to teenagers. I love horror movies, junk food, and my Burmese cat, Macoco, not in that order. The most thrilling part of my work is getting letters from kids and realizing (each time with a shock!) that my books are out in the universe somewhere and that teens read them and are affected by them. That responsibility is one of the few things in life I take seriously. My advice to beginning writers is, never be complacent with the quality of your writing, and learn to ignore rejections.

Bibliography

Books for Young Adults

1984   *Center Line*
1987   *Right Behind the Rain*
1989   *The Dream Collector*
1990   *Face the Dragon*
1992   *Piano Man*
1993   *The Tiger Orchard*

Theodore Taylor

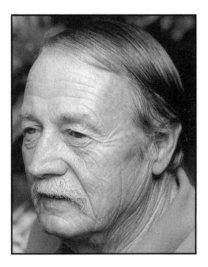

At the ages of eleven and twelve, I built grand tree houses and wanted to be a tree surgeon, save all the sick trees in America. At age thirteen, freshman in high school, I began writing, unforgivably, for money. A kid down the street was leaving town (Cradock, Virginia) and offered me his job, paying fifty cents a week. To receive that sum, huge in 1934, I had to deliver a page and a half of copy about weekly school sports events to the *Star,* a sprightly daily eight miles away in Portsmouth. I traveled each Saturday evening by trolley car.

I knew nothing about writing, was a terrible student, but, oh, that fifty cents was reward beyond belief. I began teaching myself how to write, hunt and peck, by *copying* a very good writer, sports editor of the *Norfolk Virginian-Pilot.* I tell young people it's a wonderful way to begin—*copy good writers.*

Quickly enchanted with the worldly cigarette-smoking reporters who hunted and pecked in the newsroom, the click of the Associated Press machines, the smell of the pressroom, the roar of the presses in the early afternoon, the characters who wandered in and out of the *Star,* I haunted the place and began a love affair with paper and words that has lasted to this day.

Across from the *Star* were the ferry slips and streams of sailors back and forth to Norfolk, drunk or sober; down the street was the Portsmouth jail; up the street, the "red-light" district; above was municipal court; next door, a railway station; south a hundred yards, the fishing boats of Issac Fass. Wonderful heart-beating slices of life all around us.

I advise young would-be writers to drink all the wine of life that they can, the sweet and the bitter, the cheap and the premium. Variously, I've been a sports reporter, crime writer, merchant seaman, naval officer, prizefighter manager, movie press agent, and production assistant, not to mention earlier, less exciting endeavors—delivery boy and chicken plucker. I've profited by all. Writing all the while. Watching, listening: *hearing*. In the 1930s, people bought chickens with feathers attached. One can *think* and *dream* while submerging hens in steaming water.

Five newspapers; NBC radio (as a sports writer); two wars (World War II and the Korean War); perhaps 250 rejections slips; then, glory be, published short stories for "male" magazines—*Argosy, Male, Men, Stag,* and similar others, all action/adventure, sweat, and gunfire. Finally, my first book, an adult, was published in 1954. My first novel for young readers was *The Cay,* 1969.

As I move toward my fiftieth book, writing for both young people and adults, I haven't lost a single tiny dollop of that love for words on paper that I had when I was thirteen.

Bibliography

Books for Young Adults

1984	*Sweet Friday Island*
1986	*Walking Up A Rainbow*
1987	*The Hostage*
1989	*Sniper*
1991	*The Weirdo*

Books for Middle Graders

1969	*The Cay*
1971	*The Children's War*
1971	*Air Raid: Pearl Harbor*
1973	*Rebellion Town*
1974	*Teetoncey*
1975	*Teetoncey and Ben O'Neal*
1976	*Battle In The Arctic Seas*
1977	*The Odyssey of Ben O'Neal*
1981	*The Trouble With Tuck*
1981	*Battle Off Midway Island*
1982	*HMS vs. Bismark*
1983	*Battle In The English Channel*
1985	*Rocket Island*
1991	*Tuck Triumphant*

1992	*The Ox and The Hinny, A Christmas Story*
1992	*Maria, A Christmas Story*
1993	*To Kill the Leopard*
1993	*Timothy of The Cay*

Books for Adults

1954	*The Magnificent Mitscher*
1958	*Fire On The Beaches*
1965	*The Body Trade*
1977	*A Shepherd Watches*
1987	*The Stalker*
1989	*Monocolo*

Susan Terris

PHOTO: © MARGARETTA K. MITCHELL, 1990

I n St. Louis, Missouri, where I was born and lived until I was eighteen, I spent most of my time reading, writing, and climbing trees. After high school, I went to Wellesley College where I earned my B.A. I also have an M.A. in English literature from San Francisco State University. For over thirty years, I have lived in San Francisco with my husband, David. We have three grown children—Dan, Michael, and Amy.

When I was twelve, I sold a story to a national magazine for $25; but I was thirty-three before my first book was published. Since then I have written more than twenty-one books for children and young adults. My most recent publications are *Nell's Quilt, The Latchkey Kids,* and *Author! Author!* I've written about many diverse subjects—about chicken pox and octopuses, about death and depression, about a Jewish family in the California Gold Rush. In addition to writing, I do some lecturing, teaching, and book reviewing. When I'm not working, I enjoy hiking, going to the theater, climbing trees, and reading. I love reading and rereading nineteenth-century British novels. My favorite authors are Charles Dickens, Thomas Hardy, and George Eliot. I also read as many first novels— from any period—as I can get my hands on. They fascinate me because of their characteristic vividness and intensity.

At Wellesley, I took writing workshops from a well-known poet named Philip Booth. He frequently told me I needed to "broaden my vision" if I wanted to be a writer. Looking back, I think he was saying I needed to grow up. The stories I was writing then were about children and adolescents. Now, years later, I am still writing about the same subjects. An unkind person would say that I have *never* grown up. An understanding person, however, would see I have never lost my fascination with the experiences of children and young adults. The years between ten and fourteen were important in my life. They were difficult yet exciting; and I remember them with great clarity.

Most of all, I remember the fear, fear of new people, new situations, and the fear of wondering how a person could ever find safety in such an unsafe world. One of the reasons I continue to write about these fears is that I continue to feel them. To me, these fears are connected to turning points, to the pivotal moments which affect what we do with our lives. If we hope to change, to work through unhappiness, we need to confront our fears and act decisively.

> Dear Philip Booth—wherever you are:
> I am still writing about children and teenagers. Why? Because, in a world filled with pessimism and doubt, I'm still an optimist. And because I believe that sooner or later—but preferably between ten and fourteen—everyone has to turn around, take a stand, and say, "This is me. I'm going to struggle. I'm going to take risks. What I do *can* make a difference."
>> Sincerely yours,
>> Susan Terris

Bibliography

Books for Young Adults

1972   *On Fire*
1972   *The Drowning Boy*
1973   *Plague of Frogs*
1974   *Whirling Rainbows*
1979   *Tucker and the Horse Thief*
1981   *No Scarlet Ribbons*
1982   *Wings and Roots*
1984   *Baby-Snatcher*
1987   *Nell's Quilt*
1990   *Author! Author!*

Books for Younger Readers

1973   *Pickle*
1975   *The Pencil Families*
1976   *The Chicken Pox Papers*
1977   *Two P's In A Pod*
1980   *Stage Brat*

1983 *Octopus Pie*
1986 *The Latchkey Kids*

Picture Books
1970 *The Upstairs Witch and the Downstairs Witch*
1971 *The Backwards Boots*
1975 *Amanda, the Panda, and the Redhead*
1976 *No Boys Allowed*

Joan D. Vinge

I was born Joan Carol Dennison in Baltimore, Maryland, on April 2, 1948, barely avoiding becoming an April Fool. When I was three years old, my mother discovered that I was already "making up stories" to put myself to sleep at night. (They were mostly about cowboys.) My father had a small telescope in the back-yard, which we used on summer nights to look at the moon and planets. I think that was the start of my fascination with space, from the solar system to the far-thest galaxy, but through most of my life I wasn't consciously aware that the interest was leading me somewhere special.

My father was an aircraft engineer. He got a job in San Diego, California, when I was eight years old. We left snow, humidity, and the telescope, and I became a complete Californian, with sunshine, the sea, and cats. I also discovered horses when I was about eight, and like a lot of girls, became a hopeless horse addict. I rode them, read about them, dreamed about them, and drew them. At just about the same time I developed a "restless urge to draw," and I drew constantly, mostly horses. Eventually I began to write stories about them, along with some friends who were also horse addicts. I illustrated my stories, and theirs, too; the art was always the most important part for me, and I never finished any of the stories. I fully intended to become an artist/illustrator, and took art classes all through junior and senior high school.

Meanwhile, when I was in ninth grade, I stumbled on my first science fiction novel—*Storm Over Warlock*, by Andre Norton. I was hooked, and from then on I read almost nothing but science fiction and fantasy, which probably saved my sanity all through high school. I went on drawing horses and other things, but when I wrote it was science fiction, although I still never finished any of my

215

stories. I also discovered poetry during high school; when I wrote "seriously," I wrote poems. I was in love with music, too, particularly folk music, and tried without a whole lot of success to learn to play guitar and banjo. The "past" of fantasy and folk songs and the "future" of science fiction were much more interesting to me than the present. They still are, actually, which is probably why I write science fiction instead of mainstream fiction.

After I graduated from high school I enrolled at San Diego State University as an art major. Unfortunately, after about three semesters of art instructors who were either indifferent or arrogant, I became disillusioned with art. I stopped drawing almost completely. I never took another art class, and wandered through about five other majors—unofficially—before I got into archaeology/anthropology. I discovered my love for that field because of Andre Norton (who has, directly or indirectly, influenced most of the major choices in my life). I'd read her book *The Time Traders* years before, and had been haunted by her evocation of the Great Britain of 4000 years ago. The only way I could find out more about that prehistoric period was to take a class in archeology. And again, as with science fiction, all it took was one look, and I was hooked: archeology is the anthropology of the past; science fiction is the anthropology of the future, and that continuum provides you with a parallax view of every imaginable experience a human being might share in. Seeing the world from a different viewpoint than your own is stimulating, exciting, breathtaking, even frightening. But always fascinating.

My first husband, Vernor Vinge (a science fiction writer and computer scientist), encouraged me to take my writing seriously, and shortly after that I finished my first story, "Tin Soldier." After a couple of rejection slips, Damon Knight bought it for *Orbit 14*. I was hooked again, and since then I have been a full-time writer of science fiction. It's a career I never imagined myself having, and looking back over my life I could never have foreseen it happening to me. But now that it has, I wouldn't trade if for any other kind of work.

I am now married to James Frenkel, an editor and book packager. We have a daughter, Jessica, and a son, Joshua. We also have three cats and two guinea pigs.

Bibliography

Books for Young Adults
1983   *Tarzan, King of the Apes*
1988   *Willow*

Books for Younger Readers

1983   *The Return of the Jedi Story Book*
1984   *The Dune Storybook*
1985   *The "Santa Claus—The Movie" Storybook*
1993   *The Random House Book of Greek Myths*

Books for Adults

1978   *Fireship*
1978   *The Outcasts of Heaven Belt*
1979   *Eyes of Amber and Other Stories*
1980   *The Snow Queen*
1982   *Psion*
1984   *Phoenix in the Ashes*
1984   *The World's End*
1985   *Ladyhawke*
1985   *Return to Oz*
1985   *Mad Max—Beyond Thunderdome*
1985   *Santa Claus—The Movie*
1988   *Catspaw*
1991   *Heaven Chronicles*
1991   *The Summer Queen*
1993   *Refuge*

Robert Westall

f I'd been born in a boring suburb, would I ever have become a writer?

For I was born into a marvelous harbour, the fishing port of North Shields. "Shield" in Anglo-Saxon really means a shelter. North Shields and South Shields just across the river began life as clusters of Saxon fishermen's huts. But, earlier still, the Romans built a fort and signal station on the lawe at South Shields. And just up the road, at Wallsend, ended the great Roman wall built by the Emperor Hadrian. Hadrian was still not forgotten in the Tyneside of my youth—my mother bought her groceries at a store called Hadrian's.

History? You kept falling over it. The great medieval sea-castle on Pen-bal-Crag, still full of the British Army with their huge coastal guns. Inside, a ruined medieval monastery where the stone coffins of monks were mixed with the graves of master mariners who captained the great tea-clippers which raced home from China.

At the time I was born, the fishing port was in full swing, ranked masses of steam trawlers lined the quay, sending their lovely sooty smoke and the smell of frying fish from their galleys over a town that might have come straight out of Charles Dickens. Four-story wooden buildings that leaned together across the alleyways so you could hardly see the sky. Not just a blizzard of silver fish scales, but whole squashed fish, covered the cobbles.

And the inhabitants were worthy of Dickens. Chinese laundry-men with real pigtails, lascar sailors jabbering in Punjabi, Sikh carpetsellers in green turbans, Norwegian fishermen drunk as lords, Maltese gangsters who ran the brothels. Organ-grinders with real monkeys. Even black-faced miners, because we had coalmines too. Real murders (when peaceful England hardly had any) and bodies

218

floating away down the river on the ebb tide, and no questions asked.

Of course, we lived two miles away, in the quiet, respectable part of town. But guess where I was, every fine day of the holidays? My mother would have had a fit, if she'd known. There I was, scavenging the oily shore for souvenirs, for the war was on, and every tide brought in, as T. S. Eliot said, "the gear of foreign dead men."

And, of course, we had frequent air raids, too.

All these things crop up again and again in my books. Besides them, me and my little life are utterly boring. Think of me only as a pair of curious eyes that missed nothing.

Of course, it's all cleaned up now. The coalmines have been closed, and four-bedroom executive houses built over where they stood. The great shipbuilding yards have gone, and even the fishing trade is dwindling. The river, once black and oily with industry, prosperity, now runs as clear as a mountain stream. Fish can live in it again, and the only fishermen they need to fear are the birds, the Great Crested Grebes.

But in my dreams I return to being twelve again, when the great cart horses' hoofs clashed and sparked on the cobbles and the drunks fought their flailing harmless fights, and herring gulls as big as geese perched on every second chimney and scavenged under your feet, and you had to watch where you walked, in danger from their flashing predatory beaks.

Odd, the motto of the town's coat-of-arms (which was also my old grammar school's) was, in Latin, *"Messis ab Altis"* (Our harvest is from the Deep). Coal and fish, see?

Well, my harvest has also been from this deep. And that's really all you need to know about me.

Bibliography

Books for Young Adults

1975   *The Machine-Gunners*
1976   *The Wind Eye*
1977   *The Watch-House*
1978   *The Devil on the Road*
1979   *Fathom Five*
1981   *The Scarecrows*
1983   *Futuretrack Five*

1984 *The Cats of Seroster*
1987 *Urn Burial*
1988 *Ghost Abbey*
1988 *The Creature in the Dark*
1989 *Old Man on a Horse*
1989 *Blitzcat*
1990 *The Promise*
1990 *Stormsearch*
1990 *Kingdom by the Sea*
1991 *Yaxley's Cat*
1991 *The Stones of Muncaster* (two novellas)
1992 *The Tower*

Books for Younger Readers

1986 *The Witness*
1988 *Rosalie*
1990 *If Cats Could Fly*
1991 *Christmas Cat*
1992 *Size Twelve*

Short Story Collections

1982 *Break of Dark*
1983 *The Haunting of Chas McGill*
1986 *Rachel and the Angel*
1988 *Ghosts and Journeys*
1988 *Ghost Story Anthology* (edited)
1989 *A Walk on the Wild Side*
1989 *The Call and Other Stories*
1989 *Echoes of War*
1992 *The Fearful Lovers*

Books for Adults

1985 *Children of the Blitz*
1989 *Antique Dust*

Ellen Emerson White

When I write anything autobiographical, I always have to resist the temptation to tell wild, and outlandish, lies. Like that I was born in a small mountain village, where my family toiled night and day, trying to cultivate the hard, rocky earth. We were trying to grow—tubers. Yeah, tubers, and other hardy root vegetables, for our evening broth. *Now* I remember. And I had to walk many long, snowy miles to the district schoolhouse, and do my homework by a lonely, flickering candle. . . .

Growing up in Rhode Island and being on the student council just doesn't have quite the same élan, does it? Going to the mall, working at Carvel, walking the dog—the truth is pretty boring, I think.

I never exactly planned to be a writer. I was always going to be the Manhattan District Attorney, or a dedicated police officer, or maybe win an Academy Award for Best Supporting Actress. Actually, I *still* want that Academy Award. (Cinematography, Documentary Short—I'm not picky.)

Anyway, I guess I started making up stories and, maybe just to humor me, my parents bought me a secondhand typewriter. Using it seemed as good a reason as any to stay up until all hours, so I started writing the stories down.

Time passed. Despite not always doing well in my English classes, I typed—literally—a couple of thousand pages of fiction. Really lousy fiction, I might add. But hey, it kept me off the streets, right? I got into Tufts University, so I went there, although I spent most of my time in Boston, at the movies. After my sophomore year, I found an agent through *Writers' Market,* and he sold my first book to Avon. I was not displeased.

I graduated, and moved to New York City. I figured that all of the *other* writers were in New York, so I should go, too, and—write. Go out to lunch. Hobnob. Mostly, though, I still spend too much time at the movies. Television is also swell.

But, seriously. (Oh, no, here comes the boring part.) At this point in my career, I spend much more time reading other people's books than I do writing my own. As far as I can tell, reading is really the only way to learn anything about *writing*. Also, a lot of my books, like The President's Daughter series, require so much research that I end up in the library, ruining my eyes by trying to focus the microfilm properly. On the other hand, I get to take trips to nice places like Washington, D.C., and call it research. If I have a character who skis, I can go to Stowe, and pretend that I'm "working." I like to make *all* of my characters Boston Red Sox fans, so I have an excuse to see as many games as possible.

I guess the main point I'm making here—although it's probably hard to follow—is that I've always figured that if I'm going to write, I might as well have a lot of fun doing it. Otherwise—well, why not get a *real* job?

I think I'd rather sleep late.

Bibliography

Books for Young Adults

1983	*Friends for Life*
1983	*Romance Is a Wonderful Thing*
1984	*The President's Daughter*
1985	*White House Autumn*
1987	*Life Without Friends*
1989	*Long Live the Queen*
1993	*The Grateful Nation*

Nonfiction for Younger Readers

1990	*Jim Abbott: Against All Odds*
1990	*Bo Jackson: Playing the Game*
1991	*Jennifer Capriati*

Books Under the Name of Zack Emerson

Brenda Wilkinson

I grew up in Georgia during the 1950s when all public facilities in the region were segregated. This, of course, included schools and libraries which, in my hometown of Waycross, were not only separate for African American children, but unequal.

Daily, I walked past a whites-only high school that was far better equipped and more accessible than the black school I attended some two miles or more from my home. On many a sticky, hot Georgia day, I went equally far past the modern brick and glass library set aside for whites before reaching the Phyllis Wheatley, a small wooden structure that served as library to Negro children.

Despite the limited resources of my school and library, I developed a love for reading. An accusation from an English teacher in high school (later followed by an apology) that I had plagiarized a written report was the bittersweet revelation that I might have something special.

I was second of eight children in a family too poor to have books at home, save the Bible, but I read that Bible! Like the biblical character David, who had only a slingshot with which to go up against a giant, I used what was made available to me as a child.

Moving to New York during the 1960s, I discovered the works of Richard Wright, Langston Hughes, Margaret Walker, Zora Neale Hurston, and numerous black authors to whom I had no exposure in the South. I also met authors for the first time, and had the good fortune of being part of writers workshops led by the late John O. Killens and Sonia Sanchez. Under their tutelage, I learned both the basic craft and the social responsibility of the writer. Those lessons shaped my thinking and continue to permeate my work. With the current cry for authenticity in the telling of the black experience, utmost in my mind remains Professor Killens's admonition, "It is not enough to tell it like it is. But one must tell it like it should be."

The Ludell trilogy, my earliest writings, tells the story of a young black girl in the pre-Civil Rights era who, at age twelve, works as a domestic for fifty cents per hour, the standard wage paid to black women for such work at the time. My intent in telling this story was to follow the tradition of Richard Wright and others who through "faction" (facts-and-fiction, Professor Killens's coin) have chronicled what African Americans have come through. I hope that my books inspire a new generation to continue our story.

Though I only attended college briefly, I have had the opportunity to lecture extensively at universities and schools across the country. I share my experiences with young people as testimony of what can be accomplished through self-discipline and study.

Currently I am an executive with the mission agency of the United Methodist Church. I do my writing evenings, weekends, and during vacation, and I have had four young adult novels and one children's biography published. I am a divorced single parent. My two daughters, ages twenty-four and twenty-one, have given me much insight into the struggles and aspirations of young people. My most recent book, untitled at this time, is about young people growing up in a housing project where we once lived.

After publication of my first book, I had the honor of being celebrated by my hometown. Ironically, the event took place at the very library I could not enter as a child. Clearly there has been some social progress in this country, but there remains much work to be done. Race relations can only improve when we learn more about one another. I view books as a vehicle toward better understanding among humankind. As one who writes for children, I feel privileged to be contributing where it matters most.

Bibliography

1975   *Ludell*
1977   *Ludell & Willie*
1980   *Ludell's New York Times*
1987   *Not Separate Not Equal*
1990   *Jesse Jackson, Still Fighting for the Dream*

Margaret Willey

PHOTO: ROSEMARY WILLEY

I grew up the eldest daughter of a large and clannish family in St. Joseph, Michigan—the St. Martins of my novels. Before I left home for college, I watched various siblings struggle through adolescence; I saw ugly ducklings change into swans and swans change into ugly ducklings. I saw the in-control teenager fall apart at the first crisis and the teenager who appeared weakest show the most courage. I saw depression, I saw loneliness, I saw rebellion, I saw world-shaking first love. In short, my family, which I foolishly thought I was leaving behind when I left for college, became a precious lode of information about growing up. In some ways, I am still the big sister, logging the personal journeys of my sisters and brothers, trying to capture their adolescent joys and sorrows and, in doing so, to pay tribute to my own.

My books are about surviving confusion. And about tasks: breaking away, finding a voice, learning to become a true friend, figuring out who the people in your life are who can help you. Making the right choices. Having compassion for those around you who are making the wrong choices. I strive to tell the whole, complicated story without condemning, without moralizing, without easy answers. It's a challenge, as an adult, and now a mother, not to get preachy, but I think it's crucial. I don't believe in pat answers to the problems of teenagers, any more than I believe in such answers to adult problems. To me, adolescence is a unique phase in a larger human mystery: What makes us the way we are? What connects us? What separates us? What helps us?

When I speak to teenagers in schools, I make a point of telling them that I was not a particularly successful student myself. I think students need to understand that artists often just can't get them-

226

selves together academically, especially during adolescence. I also think students appreciate meeting someone who takes their lives seriously enough to have built a profession out of it; they always seem so surprised, sometimes even bewildered, by my interest in them. They are more used to feeling that adults can't relate or don't care. I tell them that this is, in part, because it's so difficult for adults to reach back into those years, those memories, the ones most of us were so eager to move beyond and forget. It's a boundary that I can cross only by making myself vulnerable again to all the things teenagers are vulnerable to. Rejection. Peer pressure. Chaos. Boredom. Craziness. Love. It's such a challenge.

I hope I can keep rising to it, or falling, as the case may be.

Bibliography

Books for Young Adults
1983   *The Bigger Book of Lydia*
1986   *Finding David Dolores*
1988   *If Not for You*
1990   *Saving Lenny*
1993   *The Melinda Zone*

Books for Children
1993   *The Thanksgiving Uncles*

Virginia Euwer Wolff

PHOTO: TOM BESSLER

T hree things seem to have determined who I am and what I do.

One, I'm a Pacific Northwesterner, most at home near cedar trees and water. Two, I've played the violin off and on since I was eight years old. Three, my father died of a heart attack when I was five.

Although I'm a native Oregonian, I've lived in New York, Philadelphia, Washington, D.C., Ohio, Massachusetts, and Connecticut. Living in those places has allowed me to feel like a visitor for much of my life.

My years in violin lessons, and in orchestra and quartet rehearsals, have taught me things I might never have learned otherwise. I've learned to take constructive criticism, and I've learned that music is perhaps the most profound healer of human pain. And I've spent much of my life wondering whether or not the next note I play will be the right one.

My father's sudden death during my childhood gave me a sense of bewilderment that has never left me. In writing fiction, I'm most drawn to characters who are perplexed in some way. No parent or teacher or mentor or friend can provide the answers my characters seek, but by putting together small details gleaned from each of these, my characters can reach some kind of partial truth. I feel that that's all most of us can hope for.

I'm a lifelong English major whose list of favorite authors pulsates as it changes shape. Shakespeare and A. A. Milne and Mark Twain and Toni Morrison are on it. And Louise Erdrich and Dickens. And Gerard Manley Hopkins and Dylan Thomas and e. e. cummings and E. B. White and Lynda Barry. And Nikolai Gogol and Charlotte Bronte and Dave Barry and James Joyce and Hemingway.

Looking back, I'm thankful to some teachers who—although

neither they nor I understood this while it was going on—steered me to write books: Mrs. Fitzpatrick in fifth grade in Parkdale Grade School in rural Oregon, who taught me that sentences have a fascination of parts and subdivisions. Mr. Crone in ninth-grade English in the now-defunct Parkdale High School, who taught me the equation that reading equals wealth. Miss Campbell, my Latin teacher at St. Helen's Hall (now Oregon Episcopal School), who taught me that words are layered with connotative colors. Mr. Gibian, Mr. Fisher, Miss Boroff, and Miss Hornbeak at Smith College, all of whom showed me that language reveals its meanings by surprise, and that words have inimitable effects on human history.

One of the things I most believe in is this: what our parents read to us when we're little kids has profound effects on who we become. If they don't read to us at all, we'll be undernourished, with a great hungry emptiness inside.

I'm fortunate to have a son and daughter who are strong, healthy, resilient, and often hilarious human beings. My son is a jazz musician and my daughter is a therapist.

Bibliography

Books for Young Adults

1988	*Probably Still Nick Swansen*
1991	*The Mozart Season*
1993	*Make Lemonade*

Books for Adults

| 1980 | *Rated PG* |

Hilma Wolitzer

PHOTO: © STACEY CHASE

I was born in Brooklyn, New York, to a nonliterary family with a great oral tradition. There were a lot of wonderful stories told with passion and humor in our household, but there were only a few books. The one I remember best was a home medical advisor, and I think I became a hypochondriac long before I became a writer.

My first novel was published when I was forty-four years old, which makes me a pretty late bloomer (my daughter, Meg, published her first at twenty-two). But when I was only ten, I had a poem about winter published in something called *The Junior Inspector's Club Journal,* a mimeographed publication sponsored by the New York City Department of Sanitation. My mother took me downtown to receive a certificate of merit. I remember that the streets were lined, rather majestically, with garbage trucks, and I was thrilled. Despite this early success, and the fact that I was the kind of kid who read everything I could get my hands on—the dictionary, cereal boxes at breakfast, shampoo bottles in the bathtub—I didn't place anything else until twenty-five years later, when the old *Saturday Evening Post* took a short story of mine. During the interim, I got married to a psychologist and had two daughters, and for a long time my creative energy was spent mainly on domestic chores: I probably made the most elaborate Jell-O molds on the eastern seaboard. But after that *Post* story, I became hooked on writing, and I've been writing rather steadily ever since, for both adults and young people.

No matter who my audience might be, my concerns remain the same. I care primarily about the characters and the use of language. Not that I don't value plot as well, but characters I care about seem to find their own plots and even wake me in the middle of the night to tell their stories. Although I don't write directly from my own experience—the whole *point* of writing (or reading) fiction is to live other, vicarious lives—my protagonists do tend to be middle-class women or girls with domestic backgrounds, who view the world, as I do, with a mixture of irony and affection.

Writing has brought many pleasures: travel for readings and teaching, wonderful new friends, and the renewable joy of the work itself. When I teach, I don't advocate writing about "what you know," but rather discovering what you know by writing. I've taught at the Bread Loaf Writer's Conference in Middlebury, Vermont, for a number of years, and in the writing programs at several universities, including the University of Iowa, Columbia University, and New York University. I've also done some screenwriting, and have written book reviews and articles. I try to be working on something all the time, even if it's only in my head.

Bibliography

Books for Young Adults

1975	*Introducing Shirley Braverman*
1976	*Out of Love*
1978	*Toby Lived Here*
1984	*Wish You Were Here*

Books for Adults

1974	*Ending*
1977	*In the Flesh*
1980	*Hearts*
1983	*In the Palomar Arms*
1988	*Silver*

Screenwriting

1978	*Family* series (ABC)
1980	*Up and Coming* series (PBS)
1989	*Single Women, Married Men*

Phyllis Anderson Wood

So, you're an author! You must love to read." This is a common response when I have been introduced as a writer. Usually, I say, "Sure," because it would take too long to explain my actual feelings about reading. I do enjoy a good novel, but I really do not love reading as a pastime. I only like it.

Reading, for me, is a tool that is in constant use. It is essential for cultivating and appreciating the things I actually do love— special relationships, beauty, ideas, learning, and teaching. It is a vehicle for importing and exporting information and ideas.

I feel profoundly grateful that I learned to read early and easily. I can recall, even in the first years of school, being the child who was asked to help those who were having difficulty with their reading.

Even now, though I'm retired after twenty-eight years of teaching high school reading and English as a second language, I'm still helping those to whom reading has not come easily. I am a volunteer tutor with the Project Read adult literacy program.

Along the way, I have written thirteen young adult novels because I needed them in my classrooms. My writing goal has been to put the pleasure of reading a novel within the grasp of everyone. This demands a writing style which respects the maturity of the reader, while simplifying the language but not the substance of the situations, relationships, or the characters. My novels are designed to span the reading gap, to be enjoyed and shared by good readers, emerging readers, and ESL students. Over the years, I have continued writing for young adults because of responses from my own classes, as well as students and teachers on several continents. My fourteenth novel is nearing completion.

I was born in Palo Alto, California, in 1923, just after my parents moved from Nebraska to the West Coast. My father became a high school principal in San Francisco, and my mother, though trained as a kindergarten teacher, used her talents to make a very happy home. Tragedy struck, however, when I was thirteen; my sixteen-year-old brother died suddenly of pneumonia. This, I'm sure, has made me sensitive to the feelings of some of my young readers.

I graduated from Lowell High School in San Francisco, received my B.A. from the University of California at Berkeley, and then got my teaching credential at Stanford University. Later, I received my M.A. in reading from San Francisco State University.

I have taught in a two-room mountain high school, an inner-city junior high, a continuation school, an adult school, and rural and suburban high schools. I liked teaching in all of them.

Since 1947, I have been married to Roger Holmes Wood, a certified financial planner and adult school teacher. Our two sons and a daughter and son-in-law live nearby in the Bay area. As of August 1992, we also have a new daughter-in-law.

Bibliography

Books for Young Adults

1971	*Andy* (retitled *The Night Summer Began* in paperback)
1972	*Your Bird Is Here, Tom Thompson*
1973	*I've Missed A Sunset or Three*
1974	*Song of the Shaggy Canary*
1975	*A Five-Color Buick and A Blue-Eyed Cat*
1976	*I Think This Is Where We Came In*
1977	*Win Me and You Lose*
1978	*Get A Little Lost, Tia*
1980	*This Time Count Me In*
1982	*Pass Me A Pine Cone*
1983	*Meet Me In the Park, Angie*
1986	*Then I'll Be Home Free*
1990	*The Revolving Door Stops Here*

Editor

In addition to his work as professor of English at Central Connecticut State University, where he teaches courses in writing and in literature for young adults, **Donald R. Gallo** is the compiler and editor of *Speaking for Ourselves*, the predecessor of this volume, as well as editor of four highly acclaimed collections of short stories written by outstanding authors of young adult novels (*Sixteen, Visions, Connections,* and *Short Circuits*). He is also the editor of a unique collection of plays written by young adult novelists (*Center Stage*), author of a book of biography and criticism of the works of author Richard Peck (*Presenting Richard Peck*), and editor of *Authors' Insights: Turning Teenagers into Readers and Writers*, a collection of essays about teaching literature and writing, written by authors of books for young adults. He is currently working on a new collection of short stories for middle school readers—called *Within Reach*—along with a collection of new multiethnic short stories, and is planning a book of true stories about the Peace Corps, written by former volunteers. Dr. Gallo is the 1992 recipient of the ALAN Award for Outstanding Contributions to Young Adult Literature.